Words Of
A
Prairie Alchemist

The Art of
Prairie Literature

Denise Low

~~Denise Low~~

Winter 2006

To Zrinka with
fond wishes that you find
a branch to land on

Jack
2-6-06

Ivek

Ice Cube Press
North Liberty, Iowa

Words of a Prairie Alchemist: The Art of Prairie Literature

First Edition   1 3 5 7 9 8 6 4 2

Ice Cube Press (est. 1993)
205 N Front Street
North Liberty, Iowa 52317 USA
www.icecubepress.com

ISBN 1-888160-18-7

Library of Congress Control Number: 2005932698

The paper used in this publication meets the minimum requirements
of the American National Standard for Information Sciences—Perma-
nence of Paper for Printed Library Materials, ANSI Z39.48-1992

Cover, *Evening Storm Over the Flint Hills* © Jack Ozegovic, 1986 (color lithograph)

Parts of this book appeared, sometimes in earlier versions, as follows: "An Alchemy of Writing" appeared in
Tulip Elegies (Lawrence: Penthe Press, 1993). "American Indian Geography and Literature: Considerations
for Writers" began as a talk for the Kansas Natural Resource Council, Chase County, Kansas, Sept. 10, 1994.
"Another Kind of Author: Carrie Adel (Strittmatter) Dotson, 1885-1980 was presented as a talk, "The Resources
of My Journal," for Personal and Family History Workshop, sponsored by the Hall Center, University of
Kansas, 24 April 1993. "Colonization in American Poetry" first appeared as "A Personal Look at the Business
of Poetry" in *Potpourri* 10.4 (1998): 69-71. "Earth-Centered Writing: A Prairielands Alchemy" was presented
as a talk at Emporia State University, Sept., 1999. "Harley Elliott: Land Language Poet" first appeared as
"Harley Elliott: Poet of the Plains," *Potpourri* 15.3 (Sep. 2003) 1-3. www.potpourri.org/editor/features/elliott/
elliott.html. "Interview with a Kansas Author," by Linda Jones McCoy, was published in *Kansas Journal of
Reading 12* (Fall 1996). The interview took place at Haskell Indian Nations University 5 Oct. 1995. Linda
Jones McCoy is a professor at Pittsburg State University. "An Interview Conducted by Karen Hellekson:
Writing, Regionalism, Women's Issues, American Indian Influences" appeared in *Cottonwood 48* (1993): 70-
98. The interview took place in Lawrence, Kansas. "Introduction to the Art of Poetry: Some Paradoxes" began
as a University of Kansas Poetry Panel Presentation, 19 November, 2003, with Stanley Banks, John Mark
Eberhart, and Michael L. Johnson. "Notes on 'Elegy for July 28, 1994'" first appeared in *Midwest Quarterly*
36.4 (Summer 1995): 394-5. Commentary on "Learning the Language of Rivers" first appeared in *Midwest
Quarterly 38.4* (Summer 1987): 435. "On Writing Sonnets: Love Poems from Osage Beach" was written for the
Kansas City Art Institute literary publication. "Paris and a Writing Tradition of the Plains" first appeared as
a Prairie Writers Circle publication by The Land Institute of Salina, Kansas. An earlier version of the Robert
Dana section in "Performance of 'Self' in Lyric Poetry: Lessons from Sappho and Robert Dana" first appeared
in the *Kansas City Star*, 8 Aug. 2004. "Poetry of Place Interview by W.T. Pfefferle" is an unpublished e-mail
interview conducted by W.T. Pfefferle, for a website and publications project.

Acknowledgements—

The Ice Cube Press wishes to express our gratitude to the Lawrence Arts Commission for a grant to assist in the production of this publication. Also thanks to David Van Hee for the photo and delivery of the the cover image. Thanks, *ad infinitum,* to Fenna the Great and Laura the Cool.

***

Special appreciation goes to Steve Semken and the Ice Cube Press for bringing this book into the material world. My thanks to Jack Ozegovic for the *perfect* Flint Hills image on the cover. I appreciate the support of the Lawrence Arts Commission, who awarded a grant to this project.

Thank you to the many teachers, editors, friends, elders, and students, too numerous to mention, who have informed my writing, and especially the Imagination & Place group of writers and artists.

Thank you to Caryn Mirriam-Goldberg for her editorial suggestions, her encouragement, and her gift of sharing a writing residency at Rocky Mountain National Park. Further thanks go to my cousin Robin Bruner for hospitality during the writing process; my sister Jane Ciabattari, an exemplary writer; Mary Marchetti; David Dotson; David Low; Daniel Low; and Pemecewan Wesosa Fleuker.

My husband Thomas Pecore Weso contributes to my writing and my life every day, for which I am grateful.

Denise Low
Lawrence, 2005

CONTENTS

Introduction

by Thomas Fox Averill

I once asked Denise Low to draw a map of place, her place, containing on it those things central to her mental geography. And yes, her house on Stratford Road, in Lawrence, Kansas, is at the center of the map. But also on the map is sun and moon, the four directions, the wind, the cold weather from the north (grandfather), the warm weather from the south (grandmother). The house sits on clay on limestone on Pennsylvanian ocean remains. Above the house, eagles and red-tailed hawks dot the sky. Beside the house, wolf spiders and garter snakes spin and slither. The map contains past and present: from burial sites to family homes, from Oregon Trail ruts to a favorite coffee shop. Even though Denise's house is at the center, what's really at the center is place itself, and place as it has had its pronounced effects on the mapmaker. A look at the map shows a grounded person, someone comfortable with the ground, someone who trusts the elements.

When we ground a house, we are protecting it from, among other things, lightning. But a grounded home protects itself by reaching for lightning and handing it to the ground. In the same way, this writer and poet reaches out for the flashes of brilliance, of insight, of extraordinary understanding. She gathers those powerful strikes of poetry and prose, and delivers them to the reader. A booming resonance follows as her thoughtful words sink in.

Following the Native American tradition of place-bound narrative, Denise Low is creating for us what she calls a "lexicon of geographic identity." In this, she is elaborating on what her fine work has always done: she has translated the power of place into the power of her poetry and prose.

By so doing, she not only enriches her readers, but she enriches her place, as well. No other Prairie/Plains writer has both studied and written from this unique sense of place, nor from such an awareness of traditions. After Denise's elucidation of Native American traditions, she explores the creative life of her grandmother, then the traditions of Kansas and the Great Plains, then European influences and American voices, then poetic traditions—from performance and oral-based poetry to text-based to lyrical to formal. All of these prisms of understanding remind me of that map of her place Denise drew for me: we are not just one thing, from one history or tradition. Instead, we embrace our connections with all traditions, with everything from the fossils embedded in rock beneath us, to the weather, so temporary, overhead. In a poem, Denise describes an aquarium she visited with her son, and she ends with the lines: "anchovies glitter like one body/broken into a million pieces." In this book of word alchemies, Denise is able to put all the pieces of place back together.

Denise Low writes: "I always look for the history of a place before I can write about it." In other words, she likes to be grounded. *Words of A Prairie Alchemist* is such a grounding: it bridges the past and future, brings together diverse traditions, expresses both the earth of the particular detail and the sky of insight and wisdom. Denise Low not only understands the language of place, but through her writing has re-created and deepened, our lexicon.

Thomas Fox Averill is Writer-in-residence and Professor of English at Washburn University of Topeka, where he teaches courses in Creative Writing and in Kansas Literature, Folklore and Film. His publications include two novels: *Secrets of the Tsil Cafe*, published by BlueHen/Penguin Putnam, in 2001 and *The Slow Air of Ewan MacPherson* (BlueHen/Berkley, 2003). A collection of short stories, *Ordinary Genius*, was published by the University of Nebraksa Press in April 2005.

I—WRITING FROM THE GRASSLANDS

American Indian Geography and Literature:
Considerations for Writers

Another Kind of Author:
Carrie Adel (Strittmatter) Dotson, 1885-1980

Paris and a Writing Tradition of the Plains

Colonization in American Poetry

Harley Elliott:
Land Language Poet

American Indian Geography and Literature:
Considerations for Writers

American Indian people know about survival, and one of their most important tools is literature. The transmission of memorized texts, and sometimes glyphic texts, from one generation to the next sustains cultural identity. One essential strategy of Native storytellers is linking narratives to specific sites. Through stories, Native inhabitants can associate a landscape with moral behavior; history; community identity; and "myth"—the connection between human and spiritual realms. Indigenous Americans continue to preserve literary accounts, and even some languages, after more than five-hundred years of contact with European, African, and other cultures. This success is hard to ignore.

Indigenous American culture groups have distinct categories of literature, including types of narratives. Anthropologist Keith Basso, who works with Western Apache people of Cibque, Arizona, studies their literary genres. He lived with a community family, learned the language, and sustained his dialogue with elders for many years. One of my students at Haskell Indian Nations University was a member of his host family, and she respected his work. Over the years, Basso came to understand that rather than poetry, fiction and drama, of the western European tradition, Apache people first sort language presentations into three types: ordinary talk, prayer, and literature ("narratives"). They further subdivide literature into sacred accounts ("myths"), historic tales, present day sagas, and gossip.

Stories of the second type, about history, always correlate with geography. Basso learned that Western Apache historical accounts further

1

conjoin landmarks with moral lessons: "Historical tales focus on persons who suffer misfortune as the consequence of actions that violate Apache standards for acceptable social behavior." These tales are linked to places "by an opening and closing line that identifies a place-name where the events in the narrative occurred." Thus, the places become affixed to the morality tales, in part because of the titles. Landscape is a compendium of teachings.

The Apache language lends itself to this form of land-based narratives. Place names are usually entire sentences, with more aesthetic appeal than the simple nouns of English-language names. Examples of Apache names are "Big cottonwood trees stand spreading here and there" or "Coarse-textured rocks lie above in a compact cluster." Indeed, Basso tells of hearing an Apache man recounting to himself a list of place names for the sheer pleasure of hearing the names and imagining the places.

On the Western Apache reservation, because of the nature of the language and literature, both past and present coexist: "The Apache landscape is full of named locations where time and space have fused and where, through the agency of historical tales, their intersection is made visible for human contemplation." The land itself, then, becomes an atlas of tribal knowledge. This living genre of the oral tradition keeps alive the importance of the land, according to Basso, as "a repository of distilled wisdom, a stern but benevolent keeper of tradition, an ever vigilant ally in the efforts of individuals and whole communities to put into practice a set of standards for social living." When relatives are not available for advice, the land provides moral teachings. Basso describes the disorientation of Apache people who leave the reservation and do not know stories of other landscapes. I have also heard Native people tell stories set in specific urban sites, such as Albuquerque or Chicago, and so the storytelling process can encompass new landmarks as time progresses. Not all these storytellers are Western Apache, but this attention to location and associated stories occurs throughout Indian Country, even after migrations to cities.

Stories that foreground geographic location also can provide practical information about survival in a vast land, such as the *Diné* (Navajo) reservation, which is 7400 square miles. Before geological survey and electronic maps, people needed to learn navigation for survival. Some of the rock drawings in the Southwest are diagrams indicating locations of water.

Oral stories often include detailed information about land orientation, along with unique historic accounts.

One such story appears in *Diné* poet Luci Tapahonso's works, and in addition to geographical information, it reinforces the "special" knowledge that gives her nation a distinct historic identity. "Just Past Shiprock" connects a New Mexico place to a tragic tale. The title itself is a location, and then the narrator of the poem continues to give more detailed directions:

…there were flat mesas, gentle sandhills, and a few houses scattered at distances. Mary pointed to a mesa as we rounded a curve and asked, "See those rocks at the bottom?" We stopped playing and moved around her to listen. The question was the opening for a story.

What would be a casual remark to most travelers here is a signal to the *Diné* children to stop and prepare for a story, similar to the Western Apache formula for the opening of a historical tale. The narrator "Mary's" comment is strong enough to stop a group of noisy children and get their attention. "Mary" then continues to describe the rocks' color and texture as well as location:

The rocks she pointed at were midway between the ground and the top of the rock pile. The mesa loomed behind, smooth and deep ochre. The rocks were on the shaded side of the mesa.

This much description of geologic formations would not be necessary unless the storyteller expected the listeners to remember the place. Only after the setting is clear does the narrator of the story tell about a young couple that lost a baby and buried her under the same rocks that the children see from the road. "Mary" finishes the story within the story with a final emphasis on the place: "Those rocks might look like any others, but they're special." This sense of "special" is understated here, but it creates an emphasis for the children to remember both location and its human dimension. It emphasizes the site's role in tribal history.

At the end of Tapahonso's "Just Past Shiprock," the narrator refers obliquely to non-*Diné* people's dismissal of the desert-like region and concludes "This land that may seem arid and forlorn to the newcomer is full of stories which hold the spirits of the people, those who live here today and those who lived centuries and other worlds ago." Again, like Western Apache texts, time is fused with a place through the agency of a narrative account. Tapahonso consciously translates a *Diné* genre of place-stories, about a land "full of stories," into English. Loss of a child is tragic, so this is a lesson in grief and recovery from grief as well, and the assertion that no life is forgotten. Tapahonso's story is one example of how use of landmarks creates a memorable historic text.

Novelist Leslie Marmon Silko, of Laguna Pueblo heritage, credits stories with more than historic and geographic information. She asserts that stories establish community identity, and this identity is crucial to survival. In a video documentary, Silko says "The stories are what hold us together." She understands all the narrative categories, including gossip, create an extended text for psychological and communal survival. If people feel isolated or ashamed as a result of tragedy, they can recall similar events in the stories. In her collection of prose and poetry, *Storyteller*, she recounts myriad situations: loss of a child, adultery, abuse by prejudiced people, and joyful accounts of beloved relatives, successful hunters, and scouts. Silko describes the community process of participatory storytelling in an interview:

The oral tradition stays in the human brain and then it is a collective effort in the recollection. So when he is telling a story and she is telling a story and you are telling a story and one of us is listening and there is a slightly different version or a detail, then it is participatory when somebody politely says, I remember it this way. It is a collective memory and depends upon the whole community. There is no single entity that controls information or dictates but this oral tradition is a constantly self-correcting process.

Silko argues that stories play a central role in sustaining a cultural identity, especially when the maintenance of that literature depends on cooperative effort of the entire group.

Writers as well as performers of literature participate in the Laguna community process, and the location itself is also an essential part of the community, not an inert backdrop. In Laguna narratives, Silko writes in an essay about landscape: "Location, or place, nearly always plays a central role. Indeed, stories are most frequently recalled in Laguna oral tradition as people are passing by a specific geographical feature or the exact place where a story takes place." Thus, details of rock composition or texture or shape are critical to the stories. She goes on to explain that the time of the story is much less precisely noted than the location, but that the story reaches its turning point along with the specific explanation of locale: "The turning point in the narrative involved a peculiarity or special quality of a rock or tree or plant found only at that place." Plot structure logically derives from setting and prompts readers to review community relationship to geographies. The stories bind audience members to each other, as they share lessons linked to shared locale.

Finally, landscape-based stories can add a mythic dimension to individual and community life. Silko recounts how a familiar journey in the Laguna region retraces the path of the Laguna people's original migration, along present-day Route 66, and so becomes a pilgrimage that links the "ritual-mythic world and the actual everyday world." This migration route is not only that of the community founders, but also the route of a parallel creation account. Pueblo dances recapitulate this journey. She concludes that "the landscape between Paguate and Laguna takes on a deeper significance: the landscape resonates with the spiritual or mythic dimension of the Pueblo world even today."

Similarly, Meskwaki author Ray Young Bear, in the autobiographical novel *Black Eagle Child: The Face Paint Narratives,* describes a place on the Swan River in Iowa where sacred boulders fell from the heavens. This and other locations in Young Bear's book fit into a sacred geography of community belief as well as literal sites. Vine Deloria, Jr., a Dakota author and activist, writes extensively in *God Is Red* and other books about the land-centered beliefs of his people. These diverse Native authors demonstrate the centrality of land to literature.

The example of Indigenous American literature suggests that literary works are essential to survival, both psychological and physical. Native people witnessed many children's deaths, grieved, and survived. They adapted to new geographies. Written and oral accounts create not only a physical orientation, but also an inner map of identity. Narratives link family and community members together through shared histories and sites. They organize the chaotic impulses of human emotions. Stories can exceed boundaries of the known world and suggest supernatural, mythic realms.

Joseph Campbell, Stith Thompson, and other folklorists have collected several dozen archetypal plotlines that occur across the globe: the hero goes on a quest, the wicked monster threatens, the romance, and a few others. The list is surprisingly short. Poetry is even more basic: it is about love or death. Within these limits of language, writers have the opportunity to re-envision their own stories in terms of their particular historic times and places. Many mainstream writers do this exquisitely, like William Faulkner's commentary on Mississippi. By establishing a lexicon of geographic identity, writers also contribute to the vitality of their cultures. Landscape can be a marker of morality, history, identity, and belief. Of five-hundred plus American Indian nations within the United States—those that survive genocide, diseases, assimilation, and modernization—most foreground geographic sites in their stories. Association of aesthetic and spiritual values with the land, the base matter of survival, sanctifies the relationship between humans and flora, fauna, heavens, and land. These interrelationships are crucial to all of us earth-dwellers, and to seven generations of our future children.

Basso, Keith. *Wisdom Sits in Places: Landscape and Language among the Western Apache*. Albuquerque: University of New Mexico Press, 1996. Pp. 49 (categories of literature); 101-114.

Campbell, Joseph. *Hero with a Thousand Faces*. 1949. Rpt. Princeton: University of Princeton Press, 1990.

Deloria, Vine, Jr. *God Is Red*. New York: Grosset & Dunlap, 1973.

Silko, Leslie Marmon. "An Interview with Leslie Marmon Silko by Thomas Irmer" (Alt-X Berlin/Leipzig correspondent). The Write Stuff (Interviews). Accessed 22 July 2005. < http://www.altx.com/interviews/silko.html>

-----. "Running on the Edge of the Rainbow." PBS video, Larry Evers, prod., University of Arizona, 1988.

-----. *Yellow Woman and a Beauty of Sprit*. New York: Simon & Schuster, 1996. P. 91.

Tapahonso, Luci. *The Women Are Singing*. Tucson: University of Arizona Press, 1993. Pp. 5-6.

Thompson, Stith. *Motif-Index of Folk-Literature*. 1932-37. Rpt. 6 vols. Bloomington: Indiana University Press, 1990.

Young Bear. Ray A. *Black Eagle Child: The Facepaint Narratives*. Iowa City: University of Iowa Press, 1986.

Another Kind of Author:
Carrie Adel (Strittmatter) Dotson, 1885-1980

I learned how to be a writer from my grandmother, but unlike her, I have the chance to study and practice the profession of writing. As I write, edit, review, critique, and teach literature, I am haunted by the scarcity of Western minority and women writers, even today. Although my grandmother wrote all her life, and practiced other arts, Great Plains culture limited her education and public role as a writer. "Cowboy" poetry is a regional genre, and by definition it excludes "cowgirls."

At a recent literary conference in the Solomon River Valley of north-central Kansas, a woman from California asked the panel why there was only one woman speaker, myself. The men were silent. I spoke up and answered that perhaps gender differences reflect cultural conditioning toward spoken discourse. When people of the rural plains areas gather socially, men are the storytellers. Women listen, and indeed certain dictions are implicitly forbidden to women, such as boasting and profanity. In his memoir *Local Wonders*, Ted Kooser notices exclusion of women from conversation in his Nebraska hometown: "...one of our neighbors stopped by. He left his wife in his old pickup and came over to talk to me. In our part of the world, women spend a lot of their time waiting in pickups." These kinds of gendered rhetorical rules may have contributed to my grandmother's limited avenues of expression.

I wonder if this discourse style continues to stifle women writers, as well as the usual documented causes: economics (women make sixty cents for each dollar a man makes), access to graduate education, academic job opportunities (most women college teachers are not tenure track), family support, parenthood, and elder care. And so I turn to my grandmother's life for answers, or more ways to view this question. Despite the limitations of her life, she found another way to be an author.

In my grandmother's youth, the turn of the 20th century, any advanced education for women was extraordinary. Her parents did send her to Harrison's Female College, West End, and San Antonio Conservatory of Music, but she never expected to have a job. When she married, close to the age of thirty, her public life ended. Within the limited scope of her domestic domain, while raising children and running a household, she devoted free time to the private practice of the arts. She collected Chinese porcelain vases for arrangements of peonies, iris, lilacs, and chrysanthemums. She sang, she painted, she sketched, she wrote poetry and memoirs, and she read books. Her personal preference was Asian poetry, which she may not have studied in the usual university curriculum.

There was no particular reason for my grandmother's attraction to Asian arts in environs just west of the Midwest proper, and on the route of the cattle drives from Texas to Abilene. Farming and ranching dominated small town life, as well as the railroad. Even into the 1960's cattle wintered in Texas and came north on the same path, by rail, to fatten on spring grasses. Though Abilene, Dodge City, and Wichita had more notoriety, Newton was the site of shootouts, saloons, train robberies, and other outlawry. My grandmother came just after that era, in 1914, when her groom brought her north to live among "Yankees," as she called us grandchildren, and everyone else. Although she was raised in San Antonio, she did come to respond to Great Plains landscape, but on her own terms: filtered through Asian aesthetics.

In her small town, a remote settlement on flat croplands, the T'Ang dynasty poets spoke to her most intimately. She always had the deepest feelings for the Chinese poets, perhaps because they, too, lived in a landscape of endless sky. In "Overlooking the Desert," Tu Fu writes of a similar sense of space as people see on the Plains:

> Clear autumn. I gaze out into
> Endless spaces. The horizon
> Wavers in bands of haze. Far off
> The river flows into the sky….

My grandmother saw that sky in reproductions of Chinese paintings as well as poetry. Her own poetry often references stars, moon, wind, rain, and other elements of the sky, as in "Remembering":

As of yore
The moon is just as bright
Its silvery beams light up the night
As bright as day; and yet
Darkness enshrouds me.
I cannot, I cannot forget.

The moon and its power to light the world below form the central image of this poem. The contrast of its light to the narrator's mood sets up the declaration of the last line. Another poem, "Spring Returning," shows influence of the heavens in another form:

I lie awake
And hear the gentle rain,
The soft slow rain of spring.
I hear the wild geese cry
As north they fly,
I lie awake and wonder—
How many springs
Are left for me
To feel this oneness
With their return.

The springtime sky holds rain and geese—renewal of human life—but also the inevitability of death. The sense of transience and loss color all her poems, and reflect her immersion in poetry of China and Japan.

Her favorite poem was a long elegy by a Chinese father, Yuan Mai, who lost a five-year-old girl. She read the ten pages over and over to herself, and she told me it was the most beautiful verse ever written:

A friend comes with hurried steps
To tell me
That the old neighbors have arrived
To take the child away.
All try to persuade me to take the matter calmly—
But from their own eyes come torrents of salt tears.

Two days ago
There came a heavy fall of snow,
And the pools and ponds were covered with thick ice.

Playing, I tied some bits together,
To make an imitation of a bell.
I called you to strike it—
"Lang, lang, lang."
Today the ice still lies upon the ground,
But your little body is gone forevermore....

As a youngster, I did not understand how any poem about death could be beautiful, but I reread it years later, and it was indeed as poignant as an autumn chrysanthemum. It reminded me of my grandmother, and how she listened to opera every year on the anniversary of her father's death.

Grandmother Carrie loved chrysanthemums, the last flowers of the season, because they bloomed during her birthday. She said, to the Chinese artists, they were symbols of autumn and mortality. Plum blossoms evoked the spirit of spring, and pine represented old age. Bamboo showed strength through its flexibility. Each Chinese ink painting or poem told stories of human passions with flowers and trees. This fired her aesthetic sense.

Perhaps Kansas small towns are drab to some people. But my grandmother made beauty in her home. She collected cloisonné vases and a *Kuan Yin*, Compassionate Buddha, of translucent soapstone. She sang in the Methodist church choir, and she read Chinese poetry to her grandchildren.

I imagine my grandmother as a young woman in Newton, Kansas, during the 1920s, solitary. She reads Tu Fu, Li Po, and Yuan Mei between women's club meetings and choir practice. She knows the British canon of poetry from school, as well as Longfellow and James Whitcomb Riley. She once described to me how in those days school children memorized literature, starting with rhymes in kindergarten to Shakespeare in high school.

My mother later told me Grandmother Carrie grew up poor, and perhaps reading was her self education. She had read the entire Bible many times, I suspect for the literary pleasure as much as spiritual guidance. She reread *Anna Karenina* every year and sorrowed freshly each reading. I have wondered about her resonance with the Russian novel, a contrast to her conventional marriage. She lived in a small town where even flirtations were scandalous. The story of Anna's failed love resembles the tragedies of many operas, another of her loves, and perhaps this was an expression of her romanticism.

After my father's death, I found a small, brown-leather booklet in the drawer of his lamp table. It was next to the television and stereo, next to his regular spot in the downstairs den. When I opened the pages, I found it was filled with my grandmother's green-ink script. The emerald loops were familiar to me from the letters and postcards she sent when I was a child. I remember the fountain pen she always used, and the exotic bottles of green ink that flowed into her writings. The script was a true signature of her character, like the scent of her face powder. And I was surprised to find the book filled with her own writings, not quotations or poems she copied from other authors. The book recorded remarkable events of her life during the early decades of the century—an Armistice Day celebration, a trip to the Rocky Mountains, movies, and club meetings. This was a surprising discovery.

Carrie Dotson left only two other original prose compositions: a genealogical history and, in a dime store autograph book given to me at Christmas of 1958, she wrote scenes from her own childhood in San Antonio. In other notebooks she wrote scattered poems, and she left enough verse for a small volume published after her death. Among the best are her responses to widowhood:

Adrift.
The first long, lonely year has passed
since you left me suddenly.
A strange and solitary alien to life
I find myself adrift.
My last thought at night
was hopeful that you were near.
I sleep—I dream—
I awaken laughing
as I whisper in your ear
"Tonight—I have a date with a dream."
You replied one word.
"Pobrecita."

She ended the poem with Spanish for "poor little girl," a term of endearment borrowed from Spanish speakers in her southern Texas homeland. The sense of yearning for the lost husband is made palpable by the intimate dialogue with the uncertain "dream."

However, my grandmother spent more time copying the words of others than composing her own. Her own voice is diluted by them, and I wonder at her selflessness. Was she deferring to voices of authority, by copying famous people's words? Was she honoring them? Only in a few instances did she break free of her role of listener to preserve of her own voice in green ink.

Instead of her own compositions, most of my grandmother's journals are full of quotations from bestselling books of the mid-20th century and the Bible. In the front of the short family history, she inscribed the book with quotations from eighteen diverse authors, including: Lillian Hellman, Emily Dickinson, Shakespeare, Ralph Emerson, James Thompson, Hippocrates, Virginia Scott Miner, David Grayson, William Wordsworth, S. Browne, Don Marquis, George Bernard Shaw, the Talmud, Eric Goffe, and George Burchard. They swirled together into one field of thought. The excerpts all reflected her theme of ancestors, and she consciously referred to one, a Burchard quotation about reincarnation, as a statement of her own thoughts: "Maybe when you read the Lost Continent of Mu on the front pages of this book you can account for my feelings." She turned to this eccentric author to express the most personal beliefs. She never talked about these ideas in conversation except once, when she told me she thought the afterlife occurred on the distant stars. Again, she turned to the Great Plains sky as a final answer.

Perhaps Grandmother Carrie's reference to the great writers was not a passive acceptance of the authority of educated men and a few women. Perhaps it was an active continuation of her educational pedagogy—rote memorization. She describes this: "When we were little we'd have to recite pieces, as we called them, we started with four liners and as we grew we had longer pieces. The four liners consisted of such—"Here I stand on two little chips./Please come kiss my sweet little lips." She describes the "four liners" and finally the dramatic presentation of ghost stories like "Old Tompie Is Dead." From her earliest education, teachers gave verses to memorize line by line, and perhaps the painstaking copying of quotations parallels the way she learned poems by heart.

In her writings about her childhood, Carrie Dotson describes family evenings of homemade dramas and songs, and her greatest regret about growing old was the loss of her singing voice. The writings in her journals date after that time, when she no longer had that means of expression.

My grandmother did not separate literary writing from other parts of her daily life. Her address book, for examples, is inscribed with quotations, as much as her diary. Both served as scrap books, filled with clippings, stickers, and cut-up photographs as well as gift inserts and small broadsides of poems she had self published. I realize now that implicitly, along with verses, Grandmother Carrie's teachers, parents and older siblings taught her to value words for all reasons—wisdom, as well as entertainment value. No object is unworthy of verbal adornment.

When Grandmother Carrie died, I was the only grandchild, out of seven, left in Kansas. I inherited her *Kuan Yin* statue, a Bible from 1912, and the journals. In her writings, she passed on more than a few children's stories and family histories. She also gave me a pattern for how to engage with the world. Through her I understood that wise words of famous people could be copied over in my own hand and made my own. I learned that words were worth saving, along with perfumed handkerchiefs, silk fans, and rosebuds. And along the way I learned that I had an identity that I could express freely on the written page. I learned to value the private pleasures of writing.

I kept my own first journals, small volumes from Woolworths, starting in fourth grade. A favorite Christmas gift was a new diary, the kind with a lock and key clasp. Like Samuel Pepys, I worked out elaborate systems of codes so my sister could not find out what boys I liked and how much money I had left from my allowance. Like my grandmother, I put colored bird stickers in it to make it beautiful, especially since my penmanship was poor. Even when I tried a green fountain pen, my loops were irregular and blotchy. But I persisted. By junior high I had a small spiral-bound notebook to record poems and thoughts. After college, and after my two sons were in grade school, I started to keep regular journals, and at first they, too were a catalogue of books I had read, like the pages of quotations I had seen written in my grandmother's green-ink cursive. I never had her sense of melody, so pen and paper have been my voice for many years.

Perhaps my inheritance is the music of language, in the written and spoken conversations that link together one generation to the next. T'Ang dynasty poetry, with its mysticism and spareness of detail, was my first model for writing verse, and I experienced these nature poets because of my grandmother Carrie. As I learned a vast Flint Hills landscape, the Asian poets' perspective seemed an apt model. This was my starting point. Today, as young woman play sports and attend law school, I hope to find more of them excelling as editors, reviewers, publishers, and writers. I hope they, as well as men, relish the private side of writing, as much as the public chorus of voices.

Dotson, Carrie A. *"To a Night-Blooming Cereus" and Other Poems*. Privately published by Robert Scott Dotson in Knoxville, 1982. Unpaginated.

Kooser, Ted. *Local Wonders: Seasons in the Bohemian Alps*. Lincoln: University of Nebraska Press, 2002. P. 26.

Tu Fu. Trans. Kenneth Rexroth, *One Hundred Poems from the Chinese*. New York: New Directions, 1965. P.18

Yuan Mai. Trans. Henry H.Hart. *A Garden of Peonies: Translations of Chinese Poems into English Verse*. Stanford: Stanford University Press, 1938. P. 149.

Paris and a Writing Tradition of the Plains

The Notre Dame Cathedral in Paris, with spires, rosette-stained glass, and gargoyles, is one of the most colorful sites in the world. In addition to its Gothic beauty, every part of the building evokes a story. Joan of Arc and Napoleon knelt in these aisles. Igor of *The Hunchback of Notre Dame* lived in the shadowy belfry, at least in the movies. Charles DeGaulle prayed here when the French reclaimed the city from Nazi armies. This harbor on the swift, cold Seine River could have been any other village without this nine-hundred-year-old edifice and its dramas.

I visited Paris from Kansas, where I write about a very different geography, the Great Plains. In the Old West, writings about place emerge slowly. Pulp fiction and movies celebrated the brief cattle drive years. But by the end of the 19th Century, single-family farms and ranches dotted this region. In 1896, William Allen White extolled this area in "What's the Matter with Kansas," when his hometown was a collection of wholesome gingerbread houses. In the 1980s, businesses deserted the old main street for bland malls. Now the commercial center of town is in a Wal-Mart complex, hardly an inspiration to literary artists.

In the Middle Ages, the new village of Paris must have been an unsung collection of cottages, not unlike Midwestern towns. Like those early Parisians, Kansas writers celebrate their young, no-frills towns. They use similar literary traditions of poetry and prose. They remember their European forbears, who reference a Holy Land and "old country" from hundreds of years ago. These distant places are still vestigial wisps in the Midwestern-English dialect. At the same time, area writers look beyond the outskirts of town, outward to the explosive tangerine sunsets, the fringed prairie orchids, and the shelves of flint rock that underlie the jagged horizon. The grassland vistas are the revered cathedrals.

Victor Contoski, a professor at the University of Kansas, forms poetry from a tangle of influences when he describes wind and stars on the Great Plains:

West Wind at Lawrence

At midnight, late June
in Lawrence, Kansas,
the west wind wanders in
over the plains
from Manhattan and Topeka
like a violin lost
in the slow movement
of a Russian concerto.

I look toward Cassiopeia
and pray for Dmitri Shostakovich
saying:
Caph
Schedar
Navi
Ruchbah.

He describes the great constellated skies in Latin. He envisions New World land forms as he reaches to describe a mystery almost beyond words. In Contoski's work, I hear the echoes of the Catholic mass at Notre Dame.

William Stafford, a National Book Award winner, is one of the best known of the mid-continent poets. His work plumbs sod to its very core. In each poem he folds his word-origami inside out, as in the last stanza of "The Farm on the Great Plains": "My self will be the plain,/wise as winter is gray,/pure as cold posts go/pacing toward what I know." Stafford reaches backwards in time to Indigenous languages as well as the European tradition. He explains a Siouan name for a Kansas river in "By a River in the Osage Country":

They called it Neosho, meaning
"a river made muddy by buffalo."
You don't need many words if you

already know what you're talking about,
and they did. But later there was
nothing they knew that made any difference.
I am thinking of those people—say one
of them looks at you; for an instant you see
a soul like your own, and you are both
lost. What the spirit has given
you to do is unworthy. Two kinds of
dirt, you look at each other.

Ever the observer, Stafford cherishes the badgers, the blue herons, the bluestem grasses, and the rippled hills of the region. His revelry in these details renders them mysterious, as Parisians marvel at Notre Dame stonework from the Crusades.

Cheyenne Bottoms in central Kansas is not the celebrated Seine River, but it is a wetlands on the migration route of the ballerina-like sandhill cranes. Stafford's poem "Watching Sandhill Cranes" ties plains people to the heavens as surely as the Gothic spires do the French. He writes of the cranes, "They extend our life," and this extension encompasses human spirit in every way.

N. Scott Momaday, a Kiowa writer who won a Pulitzer in 1969, writes about the Great Plains from the perspective of his timeless oral tradition. His people lived on the Great Plains, including Kansas, since the arrival of the horse, and his stories go back even further, to the Kiowa migration through Yellowstone. In his culture, there is no distant Holy Land, but rather stories related to sun and stars and earth of this very region. His book *The Way to Rainy Mountain* transforms grasslands into mythic sites, as he describes the Oklahoma "knoll" his people call a mountain. Montparnasse in Paris is not a large mountain, but like it, Rainy Mountain rises beyond mere physical dimensions.

Like Kiowas of Momaday's stories, contemporary Great Plains writers still connect with the human and animal cultures around them. William Least Heat Moon, Robert Day, Linda Hasselstrom, Kathleen Norris, Harley Elliott, Steven Hind, Patricia Traxler, Phil Heldrich, Philip Kimball, Lance Henson and others inscribe the stories of the prairies. They draw on European and Indigenous traditions, and also they explore for themselves some of the last undisturbed American land. This is the sacred heart of North America. These writers build reverence for the remarkable site as

Parisians nurture their cultural heritage. Storytellers persuade their audience to look within a place and see its inner spirit. This is the cornerstone of both physical and cultural survival, for people and the land itself.

Contsoki, Victor. "Moonlit Night." *A Kansas Sequence*. Lawrence: Cottonwood, 1983. P. 63.

-----. "West Wind at Lawrence." *Broken Treaties*. New York: New Rivers, 1973. P. 57.

Momaday, N. Scott. *The Way to Rainy Mountain*. Norman: University of Oklahoma Press, 1969.

Stafford, William. "Farm on the Great Plains" (64), "By a River in the Osage Country" (229), "Watching Sandhill Cranes" (173). *The Way It Is: New and Selected Poems*. St. Paul: Graywolf Press, 1998.

Colonization in American Poetry

> "Let us decide not to imitate Europe; let us combine our
> muscles and our brains in a new direction."
> —Frantz Fanon, *The Wretched of the Earth*

Nineteenth century poet, Henry Wadsworth Longfellow was a bestselling author. "Evangeline," "Hiawatha," "The Courtship of Miles Standish," and other such verse sold enough copies to provide him the means for a grand mansion. He wrote narratives situated within American culture that were so popular that he resigned his professorship at Harvard to pursue his writing. But careers like Longfellow's no longer exist. Though thousands of people write poetry, few read it, and even fewer purchase poetry books. Today's poets may be more sophisticated than 19th century versifiers, but connections to an attentive audience have weakened. One reason may be today's poets emphasize European rather than American concerns.

The popular audience for American poetry is indeed sparse. Only three major newspapers regularly publish it: the *New York Times*, the *Washington Post*, and the *Kansas City Star*. These days, the limited resources devoted to poetry—prizes, professorships, fellowships, editorial positions—go to an in-group, as critic David Orr describes: "Poetry isn't really an open system; it's a combination of odd institutions, personal networks, hoary traditions, talent and blind luck. It's both an art and a guild." Throughout the country, thousands of people blog and participate in writers groups, but only a small group publish with literary, university or New York presses. One annual devoted to American verse is *The Best American Poetry*, but accessibility to this publication is carefully controlled. Orr describes each year's editor as "a famous poet with favors to trade and axes to grind." These editors are academics, and almost all poets who publish in the leading journals are professors with advanced degrees, or their student-apprentices. Lay practitioners of the American poem have almost no chance of publishing in the few national venues. Ironically, though, academic poets focus on the preservation of European culture more than the development of American aesthetics. As literary and cultural studies critics develop theories of colonialism and postcolonialism, their creative writing colleagues perpetuate an internalized colonial presence.

Colonialism has both physical and cultural dimensions. According to post-colonial thinker Frantz Fanon, after the physical takeover of a territory, the conquerors impose their culture by force. For example, in the 19th and 20th centuries, American Indian children were separated from parents and sent to assimilationist boarding schools. In Fanon's next phase, subjugated populations internalize that culture to the detriment of their own: "In order to assimilate and to experience the oppressor's culture, the native has had to leave certain of his intellectual possessions in pawn." American poets set aside their own cultural constellations in such an internalized colonization.

Poetry about European topics and in European formulations continues to be favored by the academic poets who control most of the genre's resources. The surest route to publication in American journals is to write about the Continent. I came to this conclusion after reviewing several prominent publications: *The Best American Poetry, Poetry,* and *American Poetry Review*; I looked at these periodicals in 1998 and again in 2004. I found that verse celebrating Europe finds print statistically more often, while American topics and poetic styles, of both Indigenous people and immigrant settlers, are still second best. This creates a European colonial framework, even as the general population demographics become more and more distant from Europe.

The form of American poetry—its stanzaic patterns, meter, and rhyme—follow European tradition more than American variations. European acculturation is apparent in *The Best American Poetry of 1997,* which, as Orr points out, is a publication that represents elite trends. This year was the height of the new formalism. At that time, sestinas had a revived popularity, as well as dramatic monologues and other formal patterns. This was a return to Continental classicism, after decades of Whitman, the Beat poets, and other American creators of word art.

At first the 1997 anthology appears to be diverse. Series editor David Lehman's introduction lists a catalogue of forms: "The book is strong on narrative... There are a number of prose poems, but there are also prayers and meditations and chants, a poem in the form of a fan letter and a *sui generis* poem in the form of haiku-like bumper stickers." The book includes a number of formalists, so I conclude that many forms co-exist. However, even the apparently experimental forms look conservative, with the lines aligned with the left margin and with conventional punctuation and capitals. Poets with ties to the "Language" school of poetry do not appear in this publication, nor do poetic forms that reference Black Mountain poetics, feminism, or deep-image leaping poetry.

Next, I looked at a 2004 edition of the same publication. In this volume, form appears to be more American, perhaps in reaction to previous conservative selections. Lehman, the series editor, chose a Language poet as guest editor, Lyn Hejinian. However, despite an apparently iconoclastic stance, this school of poetry has deep roots in Europe. Orr defines the practitioners as "an assortment of avant-gardists who take their cues from Gertrude Stein, Ezra Pound, some lesser known modernists, various French theorists." Stein's and Pound's ties to Europe are undeniable. This version of Language poetics dates from the 1970s-1980s, so in this 2004 publication, it achieves mainstream acceptance. However, their revolution depends on tradition for its existence, as the after-image of conventional forms. And ironically—though modes are surreal, magical realism, cut-ups, or stream-of-consciousness—the poetic structures are surprisingly regular. Of 72 poets in the annual, 29 use regular stanzaic form: couplets, tercets, quatrains, and so forth. About 27 use invented but very regular forms, with prose poems, which date back to Rimbaud, included in this category. Only 16 use true free-form verse with no regular structure. The poems are lyric and narrative and combinations of both. Again, like 1997, an eclectic mix of form is apparent in the anthology, although the continued presence of formalism is a surprise.

After considering form, I looked at the question of politics. In both the 1997 and 2004 *Best* anthologies, I looked at gender issues. In the earlier collection, more than half the poets are women, thirteen out of twenty-three. However, the politics of feminism are not apparent. In the 2004 edition of the *Best* annual, despite a woman editor, only 24 contributors of 76 are women, less than a third. Gender politics are so submerged as to be invisible. People of color are vastly underrepresented in both, as well as content related to their experience.

Next I turned to *Poetry* magazine, one of the longest-lived journals, and *The American Poetry Review*.

I went to the public library where *Poetry* was the only poetry periodical available, alongside *Time* and *Rolling Stone*. I also looked for *The American Poetry Review*, but it was no longer available in the library, displaced by the film section and the CD-ROM lending library. Nor were the local poetry magazines *First Intensity, Cottonwood, Coal City Review, Smelt,* or *I-70* available to readers and practitioners of poetry. Libraries opt for bestsellers and second-rate books from national publishers rather than representation of the local writing scene. This is characteristic of internalized colonialism—geographic and cultural displacement.

So in February of 1998, *Poetry* was the only library choice of a periodical devoted to verse. The poem topics in that issue include frequent allusions to European figures, such as Michelangelo and Apollinaire; many poems about the writing process itself (one-fourth); and a just a few language poems, but left-margin-aligned. There are many poetry insider poems, such as Billy Collins's poem "Taking Off Emily Dickinson's Clothes." Only a few, Collins's poem and one entitled "Shiloh," are set in the American hemisphere. The continent that most clearly provides material for these poets is Europe. No work by or about American Indian/Alaska Natives nor Americans of African, Asian, Arabic, Hispanic, or Australian descent is present. One promising looking title, "Add-Water Instant Blues" is a recursive language poem that owes far more to the sestina form than the eight-bar blues. Preservation of a European presence is an aesthetic priority. In this issue of *Poetry*, I conclude the editors choose contents for academics like themselves, who would be interested in poems that self-reference the writing process. An example is "Song of the Girl Who Stepped Out of Language."

In 1998 I looked for a less polished journal than *Poetry* as a comparison. I did find a copy of *American Poetry Review* at the grocery store newsstand, the January/February issue. It opens with a long poem, "A Geology," by Brenda Hillman, about California, love, and rock strata—all of which create more of an American context. Hillman's arrangement of four words at the four corners of each page is also distinctive. The "Special

Supplement" section features Jack Spicer, whom I have always admired for his non-rational, pre-beat musings. The *APR* material ranges more widely than that of *Poetry*, though Europe still is a central reference. An essay by Lewis Hyde about prophetic tricksters discusses writers and culture heroes from Classical Greece, the Torah, Asian countries (China and India) and, briefly, about half-way through, North America. American Indigenous cultures have numerous trickster figures: *Iktome*/Spider of the Siouan areas; *Manapoose*/Rabbit-Spirit of the Menominees of the Great Lakes; Raven of the Northwest; Coyote of the Southwest; and Rabbit of the Southeast. This tradition is barely mentioned.

A few more American references occur in "October in Provincetown" by Laurie Henry and "The Small Killers" by Caroline Finkelstein, with allusions to Lewis and Clark, Jefferson, and Audubon alongside Wittgenstein, Keats, and Mozart. Despite the inclusion of some American and world cultures, *APR* compares in many ways to *Poetry*. European tropes outnumber those of the Americas, with poems about Odessa and Czechoslovakia, for example. The feature essay by Edward Hirsch, "At the White Heat," considers poems by Yehuda Amichai, Paul Eluard, Guittone d'Arezzo, Marina Tsvetayeva, Robert Desnos, and Constantine Cavafy. The essay argues for intense writing, and the fact that all the examples are European or Mediterranean is not addressed. The implicit message throughout *APR is* that the complexities of American cities, neighborhoods, mountain ranges, social crises, mixed-language dialects, immigration, jazz, and Washington and local politics are not within the range of serious poets. In this 1998 issue of *APR,* the one African-American poet, Everett Hoagland, sets his first poem in an American diner and the other in South Africa. His American work cannot stand on its own, without a global partner.

I examined the content of the same journals several years later, and again, I found a background in Continental culture continued to be essential for readers. In the June 2005 *Poetry* issue, Europe was a looming presence in eight of twenty-six poems. Among the four American referents were "The Ducking Stool" by Anne Marie Cusac and "I Dreamt I Went to Hell with Charles Schwab." Neither ducking stools nor brokerages are high-art subjects, to be sure, in contrast to Egypt, Hades, Narcissus, Crete, Rome, Ovid, Shelley, and Auden. "Uncle Dugan," by John Skoyles, was set in

Brooklyn, perhaps an American mythical place, and Linda Gregerson's poem mentioned Nacogdoches, Texas. Lawrence Joseph's "That Too" refers to Gertrude Stein, who is more influenced by European than American thought. The dialogue between continents seems to only consider Europe and America, with American concerns set in the background. Almost half the poems, eleven, seemed to be set in a generalized site of poetic thought.

Avant Garde and surrealist influence permeate the 2004 *Best* anthology. European topics and sites—Spain, Greece, France, and their artists and writers—account for 24 poems, a third. The U.S. appears directly or very indirectly in 21 poems. Some refer to American writers, like Ken Irby's reference to Ed Dorn.

The only references to Indigenous North Americans are stereotyped at best and disrespectful at worst. One poet's narrator states, "My indian name is 'Little Hard Core.'" The questionable term "Indian" is not capitalized; the "Indian name" is a cultural appropriation; and the context of dehumanized sexuality clinches the insult. In another poem, a flip reference to a shelf of knickknacks refers to a "Kachina doll," which trivializes the religious object and Pueblo belief. The final Indigenous American reference is to the contrived and dated anthropological film *Nanook of the North*. The poem describes the primitive Other as: "an Old Eskimo [sic] with a caribou bone needle," which is an image that perpetuates a stereotype of a fossilized Inuit identity. The subtextual message that Americans are primitive and Europeans are the source of civilization is clear.

An interesting contrast to nation-specific works is the other third of the contents, poems that appear nowhere in particular, sited only within thoughts of the writers. Despite the upheavals of the globe since September 11, 2001, only three poems are political critiques: "Mars Needs Terrorists" by K. Silen Mohammad; "Song of the Ransom of the Dark" by Bruce Smith; and "Bounded Duty" by James Tate. Most poems are preoccupied with workings of the human consciousness and *art pour l'art* despite serious environmental, political, and economic issues.

The Nov./Dec. 2004 issue of *American Poetry Review* is more global than the 1998 issue, and it includes more American referents, but usually paired with European allusions. Norman Dubie, Doreen Gilroy, Jorie Graham, and David Rivard refer to diverse geographies. Dubie considers early photographs of "the nude Parisian woman" and the Ottoman

Empire along with Poughkeepsie. Gilroy's narrator ("Transit") lives with sketches of Raphael's angels on the wall, and in another poem "Hollywood" and "Wizard-of-Oz" are embedded superlatives. In Graham's sequence "Praying," poems center on Omaha Beach in Normandy, alongside "Copy," about "Attacks on the cities, 2000-2003." Rivard has a poem "American Speaking," as well as "After Borges." Cole Swenson's "The Glass Age" is solely European, located in England and France. Perhaps Rita Dove's suite of poems in this issue epitomizes the balance of events at a nexus between America and Europe: she writes of World War I, pivoting between the two, in order to revive heroism of the "Harlem Hellfighters." Nonetheless, the dialectic clearly is between Europe and the United States. Most poets do not write of American tropes without the lineage to Europe made clear.

So much elite American poetry is about Europe that I have come to look at the genre as a form of travel writing. Poets journey into sublime modes of consciousness, or they return to European watering holes. This estranges them, however, from a homeland. Vine Deloria, Jr., a Standing Rock Dakota philosopher, critiques American emphasis on temporal rather than spatial concepts. Religion centers on a timeline—from Eden to Jesus to Revelations—rather than a geography. The result is a disassociation from the land, which, in Deloria's view, results in environmental negligence. The artistic result, I believe, is a disassociation from the cultures and places of America—in addition to remaining a colonized literature.

There is no denying how use of the English language harkens back to northern Europe and the classical world. The American dialect of English, in its structures, is predicated upon an historic syntax and vocabulary. Homer, Aeschylus, Aristotle, Petrarch, Chaucer, Shakespeare and King James all resonate in our mother tongue. Longfellow wrote verse related to the ballad tradition. However, American writers of diverse backgrounds also leave their imprint in American English: Toni Morrison, N. Scott Momaday, Ray Young Bear, and Maxine Hong Kingston to name a few contemporary writers. In my region, I hear the Great Plains language and read the works of Kenneth Porter, William Stafford, Ted Kooser, Louise Erdrich, Ken Irby, Heid Erdrich, William Kloefkorn, Harley Elliott, Patricia Traxler, and Adrian C. Louis, to name just a few.

Poets make choices in every piece of writing, and many choose to recreate a European rhetoric and cultural lexicon, without critique of the colonial implications. Though many Americans' forbears left Europe long ago, it seems their descendants have never quite arrived on this continent. Poets who are not American Indian or Alaskan Native seldom explore, with respect, Indigenous people's cultures. With the increase of immigration from non-European places, the role of Europe in American letters may fade. Some of these new settlers may look around them and relish this continent rather than continuing European structures or substituting their own paradigms, in a new wave of colonialism. I hope they discover new melodies from a variety of voices as well. Though only a small percentage of poets have the visibility of a Longfellow, thousands are writing and publishing in small presses. Perhaps they can find connection with the cultural and physical geographies under their feet. Perhaps an audience might follow.

The American Poetry Review 27.2 (Feb. 1998).

The American Poetry Review 33.5 (Sept./Oct. 2004).

Deloria, Vine, Jr. *God Is Red*. Lincoln: University of Nebraska Press, 1974.

Fanon, Frantz. *The Wretched of the Earth*. Trans. Constance Farrington. 1961. New York: Grove, 1963. P. 49.

Hejinian, Lyn, ed. *The Best American Poetry of 2004*. New York: Scribner, 2005.

Tate, James, ed. *The Best American Poetry of 1997*. New York: Scribner, 1998.

Orr, David. *New York Time Book Review* 21 Nov. 2004: 1+.

Poetry 86.2 (Feb. 1998). Ed. Joseph Parisi.

Poetry 93.5 (June 2005). Ed. Christian Wiman.

Harley Elliott: Land Language Poet

Writer Harley Elliott would be embarrassed to see too much fuss made over him, and my apologies in advance. He lives a quiet life in Salina, Kansas, where he retired from the arts center. But it would be a sin of omission not to acknowledge his influence on prairielands writers. For three decades, he has nourished the culture of the region, as an artist and writer. His artwork is collages and ink drawings based on his surroundings, both natural and human history. Authentic language marks his poetry, and in the current climate of high printing costs and academic po'-biz, Harley sticks to a revolutionary poetics. He uses the language of the region, not academic diction. And he does it well.

Poets understand how every word reflects a cosmos of meaning, especially in regards to nature. The English term "wilderness," for example, suggests an environment where humankind can be lost, frozen, or bitten by a venomous serpent. "Frontier" evokes the Wild West and gun fighters. In Algonquin languages, the *Windigo* monster of the Great Lakes emerges from the forest in winter to kill and eat people. Simple words create a sense of peace in the Twenty-Third Psalm, with "still waters" and "green pastures." "Pasture" is a friendly word, suggesting nurturance of the land.

Elliott chooses words carefully in his verse. He celebrates Saline County, Kansas, and environs in such works as "Living in the Open," where he describes the space of the prairie skies as "open" and "giant":

First you lose the mountains
and most of the trees.
Birds appear smaller, crossing the giant sky.
The air is suddenly composed
of infinite dots

just inside the limits of your eye.
Will you wipe your face?
Your hand is the hand of a child.
Far below your feet
are investigating a stone.
Shadows fall
straight down into the earth.
The echo of your heartbeat
is a tiny radiating thunder.
On any horizon
you will see yourself approaching
years younger
your face
a shaft of clear light.

Because Elliott notices this "giant sky," it becomes important. Not just flyover space for airplanes, the sky is now a destination, where "the air is suddenly composed/ of infinite dots/ just inside the limits of your eye." The poet is not the center here, but rather part of an infinite web with its own laws of time and gravity. In the end, time turns back on itself, "You will see yourself approaching/years younger."

Other noted writers commemorate prairie life, such as Willa Cather, William Stafford, and Loren Eiseley. Elliott learns from these masters, and then goes one step further. He writes about his Smoky Hill region in its own dialect. The smooth, even-gaited language moves like a man walking through open country. This neighborly storyteller passes on the latest news with a slight twist of humor. He describes a monarch butterfly perfectly as a "small hinged mosaic of orange black and palomino" ("Butterfly Master"). The horse-color word "palomino" finds new use.

Another contribution of Elliott is his sense of history, from the mountain men to Native peoples to the graves of his immigrant grandparents in "A Photograph of My Grandparents on Their Wedding Day":

Ingevald and Anna Moen
norwegian dreamers
in a room upon the prairie
both faces fill
the photographers eye.

This man will die   This woman dies
In bed and swear   in bed

He saw Jesus standing   as quiet as the
On a bluff above the river   wind she moved through
And he said then   with the words
"pass by"   "I wish"

Although there are no thoughts
Of drought or sorrow
On his face

No dreams of cancer in her eyes
Tonight the stones alone
Are speaking of them
...
Rest In Peace
All Beautyfull
And Foolish Souls

Elliott populates his grassy cosmos with cattle drovers and crows and beloved family.

Paradoxically, Elliott's fully detailed Midwestern vision appeals beyond this region. His books come from presses in New York, Arizona, and Wisconsin, as well as Kansas. By digging into his deep map, the poet finds the bedrock of shared spirit. And by using his own dialect, rather than a proscribed "poetic" or "workshop" diction, Elliott ignites a quiet revolution in a literature tied to this central plains land and its processes. Julia Kristeva writes that "Poetry has to disturb the logic that dominates the social order" in order to change political ideologies. Elliott's publications and visual artworks influence the vision of writers, the people of the grasslands, and numberless readers of his texts. The poet continues his quiet revolution, amidst the commercial and agricultural hubbub of the central plains, where he is the poet's poet.

All Beautyfull and Foolish Souls. Trumansburg, NY: Crossing Press, 1974, "Living in the Open," p. 62.

Animals That Stand in Dreams. Brooklyn: Hanging Loose, 1977.

The Citizen Game. Fredonia, NY: Basilisk, 1984.

Darkness at Each Elbow. Brooklyn: Hanging Loose, 1981, "Butterfly Master," p. 98; "A Photograph of My Grandparents," p. 32.

The Monkey of Mulberry Pass. Topeka: Woodley, 1991.
The Secret Lover Poems. Tempe: Emerald City, 1977.
Sky Heart. Milwaukee: Pentagram, 1975.

II—THE ART OF MAKING POETRY

INTRODUCTION TO THE ART OF POETRY:
Some Paradoxes

PERFORMANCE OF "SELF" IN LYRIC POETRY:
Lessons from Sappho and Robert Dana

ON WRITING SONNETS:
Love Poems from Osage Beach

Introduction to the Art of Poetry:
Some Paradoxes

Poetry is a paradoxical art form. It appears to be the most private expression, as though the poet were writing notes to herself. Yet every poet except Emily Dickinson, it seems, wants to be published in a public forum. Lyric verse is individualistic, yet also it is a bellwether of social trends. Perhaps part of this curious twinning is a result of the two audiences for poetry. Poets write books for a community of readers, who will view the works alone. But also they can compose for live performances before groups. For either venue, literary historians preserve genre rules. As soon as a new poet inks her first line, she steps into a realm of tradition—with standards of rhyme, rhythm, and stanza. This tradition involves not only precedents in verse idioms, but also the vocabulary and grammar of language itself. However casual a writer may be about creating word art, the layers of complexity make this a serious venture.

The public arena is complex. American poets write in context of a capitalistic, consumer-based society with minimal censorship. Another kind of censorship, however, is lack of financial support; and the well funded advertising business produces another kind of poetics. In this mix, despite the flood of electronic media, more people are writing poetry than any time in American if not world history. Distribution, however, goes only to text products that fit the market. Because of this marginal economic role, poets are among the least visible of American writers, yet they alter the language so profoundly that they can create revolutions, such as Woodstock. Contemporary poets can practice their art within the music industry, with emphasis on song lyrics, or the book industry, with reflective, written poetry.

Rap and performance poetry are two newer genres that derive from both written and performed presentation styles. Music-based venues, like nightclubs, and audio media are part of the poetry-music category. Song lyrics follow different rules compared to those of written verse. Recently I spent time listening to Virginia musicians speak about composing songs—Paul McGill, Wendy Pace, and Freddie Williams —and I remember them saying that lyrics have to be direct, simple, and repetitive. No one wants to listen to dense paragraphs of prose set to music. Bob Dylan and Joni Mitchell push the limits of verbal content. So the performance situation greatly influences the genre, giving song lyrics distinct characteristics.

The marriage of spoken verbal art and music is natural. Langston Hughes originated the practice of performing poetry accompanied by live music, with his poems from the book *Weary Blues*. American popular singers have often used spoken introductions or interludes in their songs, also. The beatniks of the 1950s read poetry aloud with cool West Coast jazz in the background. At the most recent poetry open mic I attended, the bar provided a rhythm section, bass and drums, to be used at the discretion of the poet. Television's DEF Poetry is another form of performance, with electronic moving images, along with poetry slams and other performances that merge with dramatic monologues.

Text-based poetry follows another direction. I think of Walt Whitman as the poet who most turned poetry from performance and narrative to personal and reflective. His long, complex lines and images, creating catalogues of ideas, are less accessible to the memory than patterned poetry. In my schooling, I memorized the "Midnight Raid of Paul Revere" and other chestnuts as part of history class. A friend recited "Casey at the Bat" at Fourth of July picnics. Memorization is no longer entertainment, so poets like Henry Longfellow and Ernest Thayer do not arise in this generation. Instead, today's Pulitzer Prize winners write poetry that recalls Whitman in form and spirit. Often this poetry has a secular spiritual quality about it, creating a communal meditation, shared with an audience of readers willing to follow another's thoughts. Indeed this is a marvelous thing, to be able to read, centuries later, the textually precise lyrics of the first recorded lyricist, Sappho. In English we can read Shakespeare and Emily

Dickinson and other deceased poets, and we can know precisely which words they used. And with the advent of audio recordings, we now also can hear Walt Whitman, Langston Hughes, Lord Tennyson, and others.

The shift to text-based poetry allows for more precision, brevity (because repetitions are not needed for mnemonics), more complexity, and a loosening of pattern boundaries. In addition, the spatial arrangement creates a new dimension. Gertrude Stein exploits the versatility of words on paper, with both prose and poetry. In the 1920s through the 1950s, E.E. Cummings, also a painter, experimented with use of white space, or lack of it, for meaning, as in one of his most famous poems:

Buffalo Bill's
defunct
 who used to
  ride a watersmooth-silver
  stallion
  and break onetwothreefourfive pigeonsjustlikethat
Jesus

 he was a handsome man
  and what i want to know is
 now do you like you blueeyed boy
Mister Death

The irregular line lengths, the omission of spaces between words, the idiosyncratic manipulation of capitalization and punctuation (note there is a hyphen for "watersmooth-silver" but not for "blueeyed") all create a visually arresting piece. The verse is freed from the usual scoring of the voiced poem, and although Cummings did not receive unqualified critical acclaim, he did popularize this kind of verse. High school English textbooks still present his works. Charles Olson's field theory of organizing poetry, where the page is the canvas for a word-painting, and a line is the length of a breath, is another result of the shift to text. "Language" poetry, based on abstracted word variations, also is made possible by print medium.

Another text-based genre of poetry is today's academic poetry, derived from the creative writing workshop process. In the 1950s, the University of Iowa began the first American creative writing program, with students and professor critiquing drafts of poems in a group. The copy machine made this format of sharing work even easier in the 1970s, so students could provide multiple copies easily for class discussion. This free-wheeling, editing-by-committee method has its advantages and drawbacks, but no one denies this is the prevalent method of educating poets today—in academia, rather than newspapers or art institutes. Skilled graduates of these programs can find employment as writing professors, so the genre perpetuates itself, almost independent of outside resources. This kind of poetry often references its own traditions, especially those that originate in Europe. These university-based writers can be out of touch with the communities around them: look at the difference between cowboy poetry (rhymed, metered verse about horses, cattle, and the range) and works of writers located in Kansas, New Mexico, West Texas, Nevada and other cowboy country universities.

Whether performance or text-based, tradition is the essence of poetry. I remember when I was a beginning writer, I took my precious works to a mentor. My hope was she would praise the poems, and I would feel good and write more poems and become famous. My wise teacher would read a draft, not say much, and then suggest some poet I should read. I understand now that the gift of attention was her praise, not any vague compliments. But I was frustrated by her directing me to another poet, rather than relishing my jewels. I should have followed her advice, sought out the poets, and studied their form, attitudes, and subject matter. National poet laureate Ted Kooser says "The best advice I could give is READ." Poetry stands in relationship to what has come before, especially in the English language. My own originality stands in relationship to what has been written before me. Clichés are good ideas repeated so many times that they become stale. I need to know someone else has written about the first occurrences of moons in June and rains in Spain.

Literary texts do not exist in isolation. Gary Snyder first made me aware of the role of poets as cultural sorters. Poets survey the chaos of everyday life, at the particular time and place of their lives, and then select out topics for study. They digest a steady diet of stimulants: news, weather changes, social trends, revision of history. Then they choose what seems important. One of my students at Haskell Indian Nations University once defined tradition as that which is chosen to be carried forward into the present time. The very act of writing a poem is an act of choosing vocabulary, stanzaic form, and events. Every so often I ask classes to write down slang, and through twenty years, the change is remarkable. Also remarkable is what persists at this all-American Indian school, like "skins," "snags," and "rez cars." Identity, romance, and sub-standard transportation continue to be contemporary Native tradition. Looking at shifts in vocabulary is one way to see how language is a living being.

Poets create works that are artifacts of "historical" moments, and so represent cultural identity of a particular time. Philosopher Julia Kristeva describes the range of language traditions:

Language has "deep structures" that articulate categories. These categories are semantic (as in the semantic fields introduced by recent developments in generative grammar), logical (modality relations, etc.), and intercommunicational (those which Searle called "speech acts" seen as bestowers of meaning). But they may also be related to historical linguistic changes...

Further, Kristeva suggests here that "changes" in language are possible at the deepest level—in the grammar, logical sequence, and mode of communication. Indeed, writers often lead social revolution. William S. Burroughs' *Naked Lunch* censorship trial of the 1950s changed rules regarding sexuality and public language. Allen Ginsberg's poetry helped lead to better public acceptance of homosexuality, and Snyder's and Ginsberg's works, among others, brought Asian religious thought to readers of American English. Kristeva titles her book *Revolution in Poetic Language*, because the ideas for change often appear first in the poetry. Advertising copy writers understand this quite well, and this secular form of poetry immeasurably impacts public thought.

Poetry is made of words, and these words, in America, each have discrete histories. Poets honor the origins of words as they use them to build their works. The Graeco-Roman source of some English is clear, as well as the infusion of Latin and French from the Norman Invasion and occupation of England. Another strand is Germanic. Other influences are distinctively American, from indigenous languages of Algonquin (moccasin, moose, papoose, squash, powwow), Nahuatl (hurricane, chocolate, cocoa), and others. African words have entered American English as well. English has the ability to borrow words and fit them into the word order of a sentence and create meaning. If enough people come to understand a borrowed word, it enters a dictionary.

Each word has weight, as Laguna Pueblo author Leslie Marmon Silko expressed so well when describing the word "fragile" in the novel *Ceremo-*

ny: "The word he chose to express 'fragile' was filled with the intricacies of a continuing process, and with a strength inherent in spider webs woven across paths through sand hills where early in the morning the sun becomes entangled in each filament of web." Each word use connotes origin, its changes through history, its associations, and its variations through context. Formal or informal vocabulary immediately creates signals to readers. Clumsy mixing of vocabulary confuses the reader, while a congruent set of words sustains a mood.

In addition to choice of vocabulary, diction is made up of sentence constructions and ordering of an overall writing. Short broken sentences contrast to longer, looping, sentences. Ordinary sentence-structures create ordinary poems. Perhaps the greatest writing challenge exists at the level of sentence syntax—to communicate meaning clearly yet experiment with the construction of that meaning in language. Language poets, for example, create original word structures.

Mary Oliver is one of the most subversive and original, I believe, of poets. She creates patterns and syntax anew for each poem. The poem "Her Grave, Again," begins with this section:

I.
Late summer, and once again the egrets have come back.
They stand in the marsh like white flowers.
Like flowers slowly flying, they cross over the dark water.

And the palavering wind
is walking
through the pines

talking and talking—

not necessarily softly.

These lines do not follow regular rules, yet this is not a prose poem, since line breaks are essential to the rhythm. The opening section is more static, like the birds moving at a slower pace, and the longer lines create the illusion of slower *lento* time. The simile "like white flowers" ends one line and the image is repeated at the beginning of the next, "like flowers slowly flying." Clumsy repetition would mar the poem, but Oliver finesses the wrapped lines. The next five lines shift gear, into short lines, to suggest the rapidity of the wind. "Palavering" is completely unexpected here, a synonym for idle talking or flattering. The title suggests an elegy, and this section—of slow-moving birds the color of funerary blooms—creates the setting for a somber topic, then shifts to a riffle of lines, as though they were a riffle of air.

Oliver balances contradictory expectations. She creates the illusion of a very private moment—the observation of egrets at a time of grief. Yet this meditative poem exists within a prize-winning book, *What Do We Know*, which has wide circulation.

Another contrast is line length. The opening sets up a slow pacing, contrasted to quick, short lines that follow. The diction is formal, yet the verb "palavering" shifts into an unexpected adjective position. Oliver quietly undermines expectations of how language should work to create her brilliant revision of reality and the tradition. Oliver remasters the hoary pastoral poem into this new form and maps new patterns of language. Despite almost three-thousand years of written lineage from the Greek writers to contemporary Americans, new ideas about ancient experiences are possible and even necessary.

I use poets like Oliver as inspiration to find what unique texts I can create about my own specific geography and history. Cultural geographer Edward Casey articulates the place of artwork within social concerns: "Both work and world infuse cultural/historical/political dimensions into art." In my most inner, private consciousness, through the medium of utterance, I link to all human histories when I read, write, or listen to verse. This is a form of great intimacy and great communalism. With its contradictions, poetry practice has a dynamic energy I find in few other experiences. Each good poem is a quiet revolution.

Casey, "Edward. Imagination and Place, Earth and World." *Cottonwood* 59/60, *Kansas Conference on Imagination and Place* (Spring 2002): 47-72. P. 67.

Hughes, Langston. *The Weary Blues.* New York: Knopf, 1923.

Kristeva, Julia. *Revolution in Poetic Language.* 1974. Trans. Margaret Waller. New York: Columbia University Press, 1984. P. 23.

Kooser, Ted. "An Interview with Ted Kooser." Stephen Meats. *Midwest Quarterly* 45.4 (Summer 2005): 335-343. P. 343.

Oliver, Mary. *What Do We Know.* Cambridge: Da Capo Press, 2002. P. 48.

Silko, Leslie Marmon. *Ceremony.* New York: Viking, 1977. P. 35.

Performance of "Self" in Lyric Poetry:
Lessons from Sappho and Robert Dana

I once read that writing is the most demanding occupation, because writers are constantly vigilant about the world around them. Poets, like all writers, mine their own lives, so tantalizing slivers of reality appear in their literary works, suggesting factual autobiography. Nonetheless, presentation of a "self" in a poem or other piece of writing is a carefully constructed performance. Poets can give the appearance of personal experience in order to be disarmingly frank, or they can present narrations in third-person pronouncements, but these are disguises. Poets' narrators are actors performing on the page. They sidle into the chair next to the reader and reach for the heart, with every trick of a persuasive lover. They cheat death and pretend they are really alive in the present moment. They flatter. Poets not only contrive their lyric poems, but also arrange words to re-create new performances inside other people's heads. This is how they cast spells.

Poets create alternate realities, and the imagined speakers of those realities are gate keepers of these new realities. A narrator laments, wails, boasts, crows, weeps, and flirts: these poses are worded directions for readers to enact in their imagination. The first reader of a poem is the poet, and as the poem emerges from chaos, it creates symbolic order, for the poet, and then for readers as well, as they project their own dramas into the imagery.

Gregory Orr explains how writing lyric poetry can produce shadow plays about emotionally charged experiences, especially traumas, and resolve them on a symbolic level. This is possible because of the medium of language, as Orr explains:

But in the act of making a poem at least two crucial things have taken place that are different from ordinary life. First, we have shifted the crisis to a bearable distance from us: removed it to the symbolic but vivid world of language. Second, we have actively *made* and shaped this model of our situation rather than passively endured it as lived experience. (Orr's italics)

The simulated reality is another arena for expression of deep emotions. Poetry is the genre that appears to be most personal.

Many beginning students define poetry as "expression of feelings," with the implication that there is no distance between the author and the persona, or as they put it, "You just let yourself go." Nothing could be further from the truth. Verse is highly stylized, including the convention of the narrator. Especially in Greek lyric poetry—originally verse recited with a lyre—the first person "I" has been customary from the first recorded lyric poet Sappho, who wrote around 600 B.C. The narrator of her poem constructs a sense of space, so that this scene seems to be within an enclosed room. Imagine the speaker of this monologue as a beautiful, carefully made-up Greek woman who walks off an amphora, brushes black tendrils aside, and speaks to her lover:

Look at him, just like a god,
that man sitting across from you,
whoever he is,
       listening to your
       close, sweet voice,
your irresistible laughter
            And O yes,
it sets my heart racing—
       one glance at you
and I can't get any words out,
       my voice cracks,
a thin flame runs under my skin
   my eyes go blind
       my ears ring,
a cold sweat pours down my body,
I tremble all over,
       turn paler than grass.
Look at me
       just a shade from dead. (trans. Stanley Lombardo)

This unrequited love poem gives the narrator the chance to use extreme metaphors like "a thin flame runs under my skin." The "persona" or mask of the narrator just barely maintains a boundary between autobiography and poetry. I believe this speaker. Behind the literal words, Sappho suggests an embodied narrator who acts the part of the poem's speaker. This figure is shaped from the suppositions in the poem as much as the first person "I" and the confessed details, like the trembling. "Look at him" and then "Look at me" are commands that originate with this speaker, further creating a sense of location and presence. This speaker remains in place, across a room, long after Sappho left the moment. People are transient and mortal; narrators of poems appear to stand in place and never die.

Poets can distort their own lives to create the appearance of frankness. Some of my own work appears to be autobiographical, like this poem dedicated to my son, about our trip to the Monterey Bay Aquarium, "Abyssal Zone—Monterey Bay," for David Low:

When old sharks die at sea
they drift through kelp forests
into abyssal deeps, a cold storage
where dragon fish and angler fish
light the way and transparent jellies,
lit from within, their clear bodies
the only echo of sun. Pressure builds.

Sounds would be unbearable clatter
against stretched ear drums
but no flicker remains in bodies
as they settle into cold hell,
eyes open but at rest,
flesh as uncorrupted as saints'

while aloft, on some surface,
mussels bore through rock
and in shallow waters
anchovies glitter like one body
broken into a million pieces.

My son told me about the abyssal zone; we did visit the aquarium; and I did see these jellyfish and other deep-sea creatures in the water zoo. But despite the real events, this is not an autobiographical poem, exactly, nor confessional. Who really cares about my summer vacation? My maternal love, however deep, is a cliché to most other people, unless I embody it with original descriptions. But everyone is curious about unknown, Discovery Channel mysteries. I researched the kinds of fish, like "dragon" and "angler." I shifted the emphasis away from my love for my son to focus instead on the group of anchovies, who also have a sense of family connections, so that they appear to be "one body."

In fact, I shy away from disclosing too much about my personal life in my poetry. I wrote *Spring Geese,* about a natural history museum, during a divorce, and I wrote poems from *Tulip Elegies* during my father's rehabilitation from a stroke. Neither of these personal events appear in the published poems, but the intensity, I hope, seeps into the work. I did write about my father's illness in an essay that accompanies the *Elegies,* but poetry, for me in this instance, required distance.

Likewise, when I write about love and eroticism, for example, do not imagine that I am completely honest, but rather I treat these topics as the color red in paintings—as a certain kind of emphasis. Reading involves some voyeurism, and writers exploit this curiosity with all colors of the palette. Poetry, like any other genre, is mostly fabrication, and many tools are at the poet's disposal. I create first-person narrators of middling distance, who seem present but not located in a room like Sappho's speaker.

Representation of personal emotional experience, the lyrical, adds a sense of immediacy to poetry, in addition to setting and color. However, I do much research in the world about me as well as in libraries. I do not rely on my limited experiences as the measure of the world. That is a kind of solipsism, and further, writing is a discovery beyond what I already know. Layering the self with factual lore about the sea was a technique to create some distance.

But as much as I try to stick to documented facts, and as much as I do refer to my life, writing is fiction. By definition, writing requires omitting details, prioritizing, and arranging—and all this comprises artifice, not factual reportage. The organic process of memory, too, removes word constructions even further from reality. The work of Robbe-Grillet, which tries to make writing as objective as possible, illustrates how contrived the photographic approach to writing becomes. The main character in this detailed setting is named "A.":

The room now looks as if it were empty. A may have noiselessly opened the hall door and gone out; but it is more likely that she is still there, outside the field of vision, in the blank area between this door, the large wardrobe and the corner of the table where a felt circle constitutes the last visible object. Besides the wardrobe, there is only one piece of furniture (an armchair) in this area. Still, the concealed exit by which it communicates with the hall, the living room, the courtyard, and the highway multiplies to infinity her possibilities of escape.

This is an attempt to be as factual as possible. Yet the repeated detailing of objects in the room creates a surreal sense, as though a tiny person is in a world of giant furniture. Close-up reportage of facts creates so much emphasis that the picture becomes distorted. Robbe-Grillet uses the most distant narrative voice possible, and like microscopic study of algae, it seems grotesque.

The essence of writing is not how realistic it is, but how it creates the illusion of reality. John Gardner explains this well in the *Art of Fiction*—that the writer, through sleight-of-hand, induces an illusory reading trance or dream:

The most important single notion in the theory of fiction I have outlined—essentially the traditional theory of our civilization's literature—is that of the vivid and continuous fictional dream. According to this notion, the writer sets up a dramatized action in which we are given the signals that make us 'see" the setting, characters, and events; that is, he does not tell us about them in abstract terms, like an essayist, but gives us images that appeal to our senses...In bad or unsatisfying fiction, this fictional dream is interrupted from time to time by some mistake or conscious ploy on the part of the artist.

The lyric poet strives to create this "dream" in the genre of poetry, also, so readers enter the spell of the writer/speaker. The narrative voice creates a believable self, a drone that fades into the background while the alternative reality comes into being.

With some carefully selected, reality-based details, there is a deep disclosure of the personal self in poetry, which is a core of passion that drives the writing itself. Why put pen to paper? Self therapy? Or a passion for people, language, the world around us? How deep is that commitment? Sometimes this is called "voice" in poetry, and after the first stanza of a poem, this deeper level of a poem—maybe its integrity—becomes apparent. I judge a number of poetry contests, and this is a lot easier than people think. The first several stanzas—and sometimes the first few lines—reveal whether the writer is presenting a monologue, or whether the writer has been in communion with the many traditions of poetry. And it is easy to see if the writer has something to say beyond platitudes—if the writer is engaged with larger issues beyond mundane, ego-centered experience. Every poet writes a first-love poem. Most are so similar they become forgettable. The synecdoche, or selection of representative objects and moments to imply the whole experience, is the key. Some autobiography here is useful for realistic ambiance. Too much is self-centered.

Even if writing is not clearly autobiographical, it always reveals something of the personal self, and I use a larger definition of the term "self." This includes the "self's" imagination, every book ever read, every conversation, every travel, and all other moments of personal history. Everyone constructs an identity from this chaos of continuous experience.

One of the most successful of "self" lyricists is Iowa poet, Robert Dana. He is a master of lyrical poetry, with a keen understanding of the poetic "self." He uses an intimate narrative voice in combination with every possibility of the lyrical tradition, from the Greeks to avant-garde language poets—and then he adds new dimensions to the form. He marries essay-style structures to his lyric poetry.

Dana writes about innovation: "Part of the poet's task was to break the rules of language, to free it from the burdens of its history, thus acknowledging that history and reviving it" (*Ploughshares*). Dana begins with careful word choices, as a way to reveal the narrative presence. His speaker has a large vocabulary, with deep understanding of history. In his book, *The Morning of the Red Admirals*, Dana chooses words with full awareness of their etymology and then realigns them into present-time currency. He reinvigorates fossilized words, as in the poem "Garden Fable":

Aristoxenus, the Hedonist,
watered his lettuce with wine and honey,
knowing the difference
between nothing and something
is not just something, but something special ...

The transformation of the commonplace into ecstatic moments of understanding—"something special"—through word spells is the gift of this poet. How wonderful to revive the name of this nearly forgotten

Greek author who wrote about excesses of Persian kings (in *Bios Archyta*). Dana goes on to include related classical words such as "conundrum" and "sluicing," alongside Anglo-Saxon, fist-like words like "sodden," "gutters," "scrape," "pelts," and "drays." The lyricist takes on the guise of an historian in his choice of words, yet he always creates emotion, the necessary lyrical ingredient.

And perhaps this mixture of measured latinate terms among the workaday Old English is what makes another level of paradox in American English poetics, the tension between the civilized and the blunt. Finally, after the word duels, at the end of the poem, he returns to Iowa, the storm vanished and the sun forming a "sheen." All Dana's poems resolve in a transformed view of this solid world. "Garden Fable" is typical of Dana's lyrical mode.

Lyric poems can vary in length and stanzaic form, yet all can have the same intensity. Most of Dana's are short lines. Among them are masterpieces, such as ".Com," about a quiet cancer death in the neighborhood and the unmarked van that arrives. "The Knot," has the wonderful description (among many): "Jackstraws of frost/tumble up the glass/of my rented window"; and in "This Time," a lightning strike evokes the thought, "'they've got a nuke.'" This is the American lyric poem as its original best.

And then Dana has another lyrical form. He writes: "I want to push on past my 'style' to some new way of seeing and hearing and talking. To invoke a new rhythm, a new timing. For a very long time, I've wanted a poetry that was less compositional and more improvisational. Less predictable." Thus the word-wizard sets off into a new maze. The rest of *The Morning of the Red Admirals* is either prose or prose-influenced verse. Not narrative and not exactly prose poems, these pieces derive from the lineage of the essay.

"In Panama," the second section, establishes the relationship of poetry to the essay genre. It ambles from topic to topic—the tropics, lepidoptery, Greek myth, poetry writing—but brings all ideas together to reflect on composition. The central metaphor is the erratic flight of the red admiral butterfly, which improvises "the order of its strokes freshly every time, never repeating itself." This parallels the unstructured course of the essay itself: "Look for me, Reader, in the dapple of these lines." The remaining poems, in the final section, "Ten Thousand Wingbeats Five Hundred Heartbeats," proceed in fresh structures, never repeating themselves.

Among the best of these is "Stepping Lightly," which also perambulates through ideas of transience. It begins with reference to the renewal of time: "This day is the edge we live on." The long lines shift across the page, in the style of Charles Olson's visual field composition. Thoughts progress like an open-ended exploration, in associations rather than Aristotelian measures. These are not Robert Bly's "leaps" so much as "essays," or attempts at knowledge.

Dana's own Iowa landscapes still interact with the work but in oblique reflections, as in "This morning, spring snow bundles the woods," and "'Who are you? And you?'/I want to ask the faces behind the windows of passing cars, /The walkers on streets and in parking lots,/ The girl at the Target checkout." Lines are freed from grammatical completeness, as the poem is freed from classical coherence. Fragmentary images hang suspended in the matrix of the poem: "Woe unto the joy and magic of our small cat./Black-grey and white mischief." After description of the cat who "speaks a language of one coarse syllable," the poet raises the grand theme of mortality, the cat's "sudden cancer," Dana ends with a flourish:

I'm off now,
Down
some moonless fractal, wild refraction, unpredictable reflection.
Starless.
Stepping lightly.

The last lines appear to be spoken by the poet himself, a man in his seventies, but this person is a narrator who pulls even young readers into the drama. The narrative voice is so close to the subject matter—human consciousness—that specific characteristics of the author collapse into universalities. "Fractal" may be the word that best describes the lines here, a contour of a coastline or other organic border.

Writer Phillip Lopate extols the essay form, which "allows you to ramble in a way that reflects the mind at work …. In an essay the track of a person's thoughts struggling to achieve some understanding of a problem is the plot, is the adventure." Dana takes this lesson of the essay and transfers it to lyrical poetry.

Dana's poems reflect history, and they enter the immediate moment. He reviews fragments of his personal and communal experience, and then selects the most appropriate pieces to construct a better reality. Such composition, connecting past and present, takes mature control of language, as well as ego. What "track" of a person's thoughts is valuable to others? And what is self-indulgent? This master of words, and of life, knows the answer to this crucial question. He performs sidesteps, sashays, reversals, and deep bends in his word-dance to engage the reader as a partner. This enlarges his own self into a hero, as Orr describes:

> It is in the context of the personal lyric and its subset, the transformative lyric, that certain figures emerge; poets who, coping with their own crises and traumas, seized the opportunity to create new selves and new meanings through the makings of poems. These poets became poet-heroes by disclosing visionary possibilities that went far beyond their own private situations and revealed hopes and meanings that were broadly useful to others, both contemporaries and those of us who came after. (139)

Our sense of self shifts as we speak and perform different roles, even in the not-quite-real world of writing. J.L. Austin writes about this idea of identity as "performativity." The role that is performed becomes the self:

> It is a doing that constitutes a being, an activity that creates what it describes. Performatives are intelligible only within a matrix that is simultaneously social and semiotic. "I pronounce you man and wife" both performs an action and describes a new state of being.

Language merges with physical action. New possibilities of the self arise in the act of such writing/performing. William Stafford specifically describes the extension of self that occurs in the act of writing: "A writer is not so much someone who has something to say as he is someone who has found a process that will bring about new things he would not have thought of if he had not started to say them." He emphasizes the "new things" that appear in this process, and how the act creates his identity as a writer—someone always inventing himself.

Part of the expansion of self through the writing process is association with the literary tradition. The structures of poetry—of language and of its history—arise in the words I write, and my simple self becomes enlarged to participate in a tradition that is as old as human speech. Poetry becomes a collective memory, and my personal experience interacts with the etymology of each word, with each connotation, with every turn of phrase.

I distinguish these ideas from T.S. Eliot's in "Tradition and the Individual Talent," because I think that although Eliot writes about a "continual surrender" of the poet's self" and "continual self-sacrifice," there is more for the writer than becoming "the shred of platinum" that is a catalyst. I do not believe Eliot's idea that the writer is an inert medium, and that poetry "is not the expression of personality, but an escape from personality." The "self" revealed as I write is an exciting possibility of my personality, now enacted, that I would nave never discovered without writing. I think I become a better poet when I perform ideas beyond my own autobiography, and beyond "surrender."

So when I visit a sea aquarium and my son tells me his idea about the deepest part of the bay, where flesh does not decompose, and how he thinks there must be a shark and whale morgue down there, that image triggers a larger process. I love learning this knowledge from him, and spending time exploring a bay. This memory, though, has more than one life. Like Dana, I can re-create it in lyric poetic forms; I can wrap it into this essay, and I can recite it to an audience. Each time I read or speak the poem, it has a set narrator, somewhat familiar, and each time, I meet the words in new ways, and discover a new "self."

Hedges, Warren. "Performative." Southern Oregon University English Dept. Accessed 10 June 2005. http://www.sou.edu/English/IDTC/Terms/terms.htm#anchor42031

Dana, Robert. *The Morning of Red Admirals*. Tallahassee: Anhinga, 2004. Pp. 19; 9; 37-38; 67-70.

-----. "Refracted Light: Life as Text. *Ploughshares* 54 (Spring 1991). <http://www.pshares.org/issues/article.cfm?prmArticleID=2988>

Eliot, T.S. "Tradition and the Individual Talent."

Gardner, John. *The Art of Fiction: Notes on Craft for Young Writers*. Rpt. 1984. New York: Vintage, 1985. P. 97

Lopate, Phillip. "The Essay Lives—in Disguise." *New York Times Book Review* 18 Nov. 1984: 1+. P. 47.

Low, Denise. *New and Selected Poems 1979-1999*. Lawrence: Penthe, 1999.

Orr, Gregory. *Poetry as Survival*. Athens: University of Georgia Press, 2002. Pp. 4-5; 139.

Robbe-Grillet, Alain. *Voyeur*. 1955. Trans. Richard Howard. New York: Grove, 1958.

Sappho. *Poems*. Trans. Stanley Lombardo. Indianapolis: Hackett, 2002.

Stafford, William. "On Writing." *Writing the Australian Crawl*. Ann Arbor: University of Michigan Press.

On Writing Sonnets:
Love Poems from Osage Beach

Osage Beach Sonnets

For Tom

1.

Time collapses as we walk mountains
and find hand-worked chert edges
among the jumble of wrecked boulders.
Form shatters into chips, reforms into use,
falls away again into broken bird points.
The afternoon stretches into a labyrinth:

which path around that scrub oak?
What turns before we leave this day?
A new moment arises among geodes
at our feet—crystals folded into matrix.
We find surprise cupped in our hands,
like a rockslide caught against slope,

stones eroding into gritty grasslands
where fits—the lush wet print of a cougar.

2.

We walk through knives, step carefully
as we speak, breathe with the mountains
as they rise and fall, old *Aux-Arcs.*
Chert—alabaster white and luminous
against dirt; blocky chunks and blades
scattered; accidentals lost among tree roots.

Some veins of the stone giant run red
as our own blood. Ferrous seams

break underfoot, a beast's rock spine,
as rosy as ruddy lips and gums and palms.
We are rouged by the same mother
as this expanse of Cambrian boulders.

Several steel-gray flints, too, fell from stars
millennia ago, onto this color-filled planet.

3

From the young Colorado mountains
great steps lead eastward and downward
to spread of silty plains among foothills,
into oak savannahs and coal beds, deeper,
farther back into the worlds before this one
with simpler life forms—mussels—and then

silence in the stone tombs underfoot.
We walk through catacombs of time
this spring afternoon, near each other,
far from each other, small streambeds
for trails, no wind but then some crows,
deer tracks, and a distant panther chokes.

On the rocky hike back, this could be the day
we first met. Or the day this world began.

4.

Placid river country, yet flint nodules rest
among limestone sea bottoms, inexplicable,
glassy among the porous tangles of shells
and ferns and crinoids. Storms unearth
campsites laid over ancient wreckage,
spring rains laving extinguished hearths

and thousand-year-old tools. We stop
as two geese part the clouds and speak.

Below, we find a woman's hide scraper,
bone-white, hand-sized, and decide whether
to leave it to the run-off or carry it farther
into this world. Far from oceans

we move more slowly, see long horizons,
turn to the sky for tides of light and dark.

OZARK MOUNTAIN INSPIRATION

These poems began with a spring visit to the Ozarks. The weather was just warm enough to walk outdoors, yet no other travelers were about. My husband and I stopped at Osage Beach, watched beaver and geese in a small lake, and then hiked downhill to a remarkable site, mounded and strewn with natural cairns. The broken mountain created its own pattern of disintegration, and I recalled artist Robert Smithson's observation, "There's always a sense of highly developed structures in the process of disintegration." He suggested the term "entropology," rather than entropy, to denote the study of disintegrating ruins.

The lower slope dropped steeply into Lake of the Ozarks, so water reflected the stony landscape as even more broken than the originals. Time collapsed as we walked among the geologic forms. We became shadows of light sweeping across the mountain for a brief instant. We lost the blinders of human perspective and focused on rocks and their slow, hard persistence through the ages. I remembered the poet Theodore Enslin once wrote, "Rocks are alive, just at a different speed," and we slowed our pace. Among these Cambrian and Pre-Cambrian rocks, the oldest on the planet, primal matter is a graspable fact. I thought about theories of meteorites and the origin of life. We also found flint, or chert, and my husband identified an artifact, a scraper; so other layers of history crisscrossed the mountainside. Osage people, who once lived in earthen mounds, occupied this area for many years before Cherokee bands arrived, in the 1700s, and then waves of European American settlers. This density of histories inspires me.

Later, as we returned to the car, we found a large animal track, freshly made, that could have been a cougar's. Cougars, or mountain lions, and panthers are making a comeback in my home, the northeast Kansas area, and also in nearby Missouri Ozarks, so this is not a fanciful guess. Nature is a living presence, fanged and clawed. Trips like this one to the Ozark Mountains inspire my writing process, because fewer layers are between me and the land's reality. The geological epochs are frozen tableaux, with volcanic activity and other processes stopped in place, freeze-framed. As we walked, my husband and I had the sense we were walking through the inside of a paralyzed volcano.

I always look for the history of a place before I can write about it, and after this trip, I read about the Ozarks, or *Aux Arcs* as the first French traders called the area, since the domed mountains seem like land-arcs to them. These are heavily weathered mountains, almost worn away, with some of the oldest outcroppings of inner-earth rocks. Poetry prompts me to look outwardly, to visit places outside my usual expectations, like these folded and creased hillocks—the "ruins" of this planet—and then to research them, think, and internalize the ideas.

LYRIC INTENSITY AND LANGUAGE

As I thought about the Ozark Mountains, I experienced how writing, like all art genres, expresses a unique human consciousness. In addition to self-awareness, we have abstract languages. Sometimes I envy other species that do not have this burden of imperfect narratives. The birds in my backyard feeder seem focused on their activities without the compulsion I have to construe complications. They do not appear to worry; they do not record histories; they do not make ceremonies. Rather, they focus on perceptions of the world around them.

The best poetry uses words to simulate direct experiences of the senses, emotions, and intellect. Human brains have areas similar to reptiles and mammals, as well as the unique cerebral cortex, or front brain. The synergy among these can create a transcendent awareness. I am attracted to text and other art objects that show pathways to this transcendent state. This dimension is beyond language, and so is especially hard to express, as the *Tao Te Ching* says: that which can be spoken is not the true way. Visual and musical arts speak more directly to the brain. Words are trickier, as language translates into meaning more slowly than visual images or musical notes. For example, look at the symbol + and then read the three-syllable word "positive." The symbol transfers meaning much more quickly. This biological apparatus of eye-brain coordination is what writers have to consider. What combination of words can confuse the mind into creating a simulated reality? How many levels of meaning can be packed into a burst of sound or text?

When I write, I feel something in my heart; my fingers have tactile involvement; my mind forms images; and my inner ear assembles sound-echoes. If I am lucky, I connect with something else—wisps of intuition—and I can plumb the subconscious. Sometimes I get physically thirsty when I write, as though I need more water to become a better conductor of electrical impulses.

Language is a way to organize nearly inexplicable experiences like this Ozark sojourn, and specifically the highly ritualized, ordered language like the sonnet pattern is appropriate. A nonverbal state of entrancement, on the one hand, compressed into the fourteen-line word container, on the other hand, is an interesting paradox. Experience is a floating butterfly evading a mesh net. The tension between chaotic reality and grammatical order creates the energy of verse.

I returned from the Ozark trip with a pocketful of stones, which I arranged in rows, dated, and labeled. The intangible memories I organized into a mental collector's drawer, the sonnet.

Lyric Possibilities of the Sonnet Form

I have read sonnets from my earliest schooling in poetry. Shakespeare's sonnets astonish me with logical progressions that entrap images like morsels in an orb spider's web, as in sonnet 116:

Let me not to the marriage of true minds
Admit impediments, love is not love
Which alters when it alteration finds,
Or bends with the remover to remove.
O no, it is an ever-fixed mark
That looks on tempests and is never shaken;
It is the star to every wand'ring bark,
Whose worth's unknown, although his height be taken.
Love's not Time's fool, though rosy lips and cheeks
Within his bending sickle's compass come.
Love alters not with his brief hours and weeks,
But bears it out even to the edge of doom:
If this be error and upon me proved,
I never writ, nor no man ever loved.

Shakespeare imagines a star, "as an ever-fixed mark,/that looks on tempests and is never shaken," so the poet represents this star as the fixity of true love. Perhaps this is the navigator's North Star, as "It is the star to every wandering bark." Shakespeare altered the Italian version of the "little song" to be fourteen lines, abab, cdcd, efef, gg, with the first eight lines presenting a problem, the next four a possible resolution, and the final couplet a slantways conclusion. More than line and rhyme pattern, the sonnet is a sequence of problem and solution.

Not all sonnets must conform to exact historic patterns. I read William Stafford's shorter poems as variants of the fourteen-line sonnet form. For example, his poem "For a Distant Friend" has twelve lines but acts very much like a sonnet:

Where Western towns end nobody cares,
finished things thrown around,
prairie grass into old cars, a lost race
reported by tumbleweed.

And hints for us all stand there, small
or shadowed. You can watch
the land by the hour, what hawks overlook,
little things, grain of sand.

But when the right hour steps over the hills
all the sage flashes at once,
a gesture for miles to reach every friend:
Yes. Though there's wind in the world.

This poem paints a picture of desolation in the Great American Desert: abandoned cars overgrown by grass; tumbleweeds; and hawks that "overlook." After the first two quatrains, the poem turns, using the conjunction "but" to signal this shifting gear. The mood of isolation dissolves, and the landscape becomes animated with living beings that welcome observers, the "us" in the poem. "Sage flashes" in the sun, which the narrator describes as a "gesture" to "every friend." This leads to the generalized affirmation: "Yes." However, the transition to friendly hills and plants is not complete. The last line reverses yet again, to remind the reader of "wind in the world," returning to the desolation of the opening stanzas. This last line enacts the role of the final couplet in a Shakespearean sonnet, with recapitulation and also a progressive conclusion.

Poet Gerald Stern celebrates possible sonnet variations in his essay "Thoughts on the Sonnett," using the Italian spelling. He comments on sonnets by Gerard Manley Hopkins, which are ten-and-a-half lines, and his own, made of twenty lines. He sees the fourteen-line form as an intention more than a strict pattern:

> In answer to the question, why is it a "sonnet" then, one answer could be that it *feels* like a sonnet, or it works like a sonnet, or it has the strategies of a sonnet, and the poet knows he is composing in a seven-hundred-year old tradition. Also it is a sonnet because of the extreme subjectivity, the reconciliation of opposites, the extensive use of argument, and its nature to illuminate, though not only sonnets do these things, nor do all sonnets.

So Stern considers the "intention," the "feel" and the tradition. I like his comment on "reconciliation of opposites," which to me is the center of the form, exactly the moment and location of the reversal or "*volta*." Stafford reconciles bleak isolation to fitting into nature.

Other contemporary writers take the idea of a sonnet and adapt it to new language situations. Molly Peacock describes the American sonnet as a "skeleton," rather than a "container or prison" (quoted in Ryan). Kate Ryan expands the idea of this "skeleton" as a living structure: "I can see a beautiful, animated x-ray of a galloping horse. This is a muscular and vigorous feeling about form." Sonnets are long enough to describe, explain, turn, and make a final leap at the end, so suggestion of narrative is part of the sonnet form as well. They recollect riddles, with the same buildup to the final solution. But always, the brevity allows lyric intensity.

For me, no discussion of sonnets is complete without a look at Rilke's sonnets, composed in the 1920s. These verses especially are inspiring, because he creates a fully engaged consciousness, with many layers of literal and transcendent meanings. He organizes his sonnets into two quatrains followed by two tercets. He twists images into unexpected shapes, as in the opening image of this sonnet:

> O dancer: your steps translating
> all vanishing into act: What lines they traced!
> And the final spin, that tree of motion,
> did it not whirl into itself the fleeting year? (II 18)

Here, the dancer's steps are words of a translator; the vertical human "spin" becomes a "tree of motion," recalling the tree of the collection's opening sonnet ("A tree arose!"); the "spin" is also a circular "whirl"; and finally, the universal visual symbol of a spiral becomes time, the "fleeting year." He works with dense, unexpected imagery—tree, dance, spiral, and time—overwhelming the rational processes so that another kind of multi-faceted yet simultaneous perception occurs. Rilke evokes the metaphysical with his fresh use of the universal symbol of circles. Poet Gregory Orr asserts that "Because they embody perfection, circles and spheres are frequent images of divine order." However intense the poem, the literal level of meaning is always clear, in each application. Orr goes on to declare sacred poetry as that which "imagines order as 'up there' (in the sky, in heaven, above the earth) or 'over there' (beyond the door of death)." Rilke takes advantage of all possibilities of the sacred with his use of the spiral in this sonnet.

Rilke accomplishes so much in fourteen lines. His four stanzas sustain emotions, yet also allow for intellectual complexity. In this sonnet addressed to the dancer, the images accumulate and create overtones, like those of the throat singers of Tuva, so one vibrating image ignites the entire experience. This creates a weighty, ceremonial pace, with the careful lines measured like directed steps in a dance, with a pause and a turn and the beat of the next line. Each phrase has momentum to reorder the universe, with the lines made as tangibly as strata of sediments.

I had been rereading Rilke's sonnets when I began writing these four interlocking pieces. Since I write in an American dialect, with borrowings from languages that are not Indo-European, the strict Italian or Shakespearean sonnet rhymes are strained. So I submerged the rhyme schemes and, rather, looked for clusters of similar sounds, emphasized with repetitions and pacing. This form adapts to new uses, perhaps because it meets the needs of human short-term and long-term memory. It reflects a human need for ordered passion.

Orr, Gregory. *Poetry as Survival.* Athens: University of Georgia Press, 2002. Pp. 209; 211.

Rilke, Rainer Maria. Trans. Edward Snow. *Sonnets to Orpheus.* New York: North Point Press, div. Farrar, Straus and Giroux, 2004.

Ryan, Kate. "I Go to AWP." *Poetry* 186.4 (July/August 2005): 343-57. P. 349.

Smithson, Robert. *The Writings of Robert Smithson.* New York: New York University Press, 1979. P. 187.

Stafford, William. *Kansas Poems of William Stafford.* Ed. Denise Low. Topeka: Woodley: 1990. P. 12.

Stern, Gerald. "Thoughts on the Sonnet." Norton Poets Online 2 (April 2002). Accessed 14 July 2005. < http://www.nortonpoets.com/archive/020419.htm>

II—SPEAKING THE LANGUAGE OF PLACE

Impact of Poetry of Place Interview, by T.F. Pferrle

Cottonwood Review Interview, by Karen Hellekson:
Writing, Regionalism, Women's Issues, American Indian Influences

Notes on the Poem "Elegy for July 28, 1994"

Comment for "Learning the Language of
Rivers" (Midwest Quarterly)

"Interview with a Kansas Author," by Linda Jones McCoy:
Prairie and American Indian Influences, The Business of Writing and Teachers

Impact of Place in Poetry:
Interview by W.T. Pfefferle

W.T. Pfefferle: How do you think places, the places you've lived and worked, impact your poetry?

Denise Low: I love to travel, and I love to return home to Kansas. For almost thirty years I have written about this recursive motion of outward observation and inward reorganization of consciousness. Because I also have lived in the same house thirty years, I have a fixed location for "home." I know the dimension of time in one set place. The poem "Fallacy of Travel" is a response to a friend who left high school early to move to Ojai, California:

Here in the center of fields
and low hills, where surf crashes
only in fossil limestone,
the great silence around me

is a lie. After twenty years
I finally know, Bruce,
I was not left behind.
This shelf of rock soars

through wind and sine waves
of time. I watch buildings
appear and collapse. Trees
I planted stretch up and fall
There is a noise, too,
I hear in bed at night,

a drone deeper than cicadas.
I hold my husband close.

We read Rilke together
and listen to squirrels
thud on the roof and apples
fall and our brass bed,

on casters, rolls forward
at the speed of starlight
and the walls move, too,
at the same speed, fast,

much too fast,
and this only seems solid,
this moon-framed night, here,
as I remember you.

I have never lived more than a hundred miles from my birthplace, which is within sight of the Flint Hills of Kansas. The sky and angular stone vistas suggest possibilities; they tantalize; they provide a proscenium for the imagination. The horizon line blurs into an electric-blue energy that is neither air nor earth, but rather an indeterminate element. Sunsets blare sky-fulls of cerise or tangerine or brooding night-sea black. Gales or deluges or desert-hot lights fill the sky. Even killer blizzards bring displays of crystalline optics. This daily drama whetted my sense of aesthetics when I was young, and it engages me today. If I had been born with patience and hand-eye coordination, I would have become an artist.

I am a failed painter and a failed traveler: I always return and I am always tongue-tied. I express myself more easily in writing than speaking. Only words redeem the sense of loss when I return from a weekend in the Flint Hills. In writing, I retrieve the sense of stillness seen beyond cumulus and cirrus formations. I reconcile myself to calibrations of verbs and adjectives. The most important goal in my writing is to access language that reactivates experience of such extremes. This goal is unobtainable, but it draws me forward.

Because I live in grasslands, boundaries are not clearly defined, and so more room exists for imagination. The river at the edge of town is visible only in the traces of cottonwood branches along its outline, and so the suggested river is as interesting as the one discovered on a walk. This geography and the prairielands American-English dialect shape my poetry.

Like another Kansan poet, William Stafford, I am preoccupied with time. The exposed land formations suggest cosmic epochs. I find myself referring to geology and myth and history of the grasslands to represent the layers of time in the poem "Flint Hills Sunset, Spring Equinox":

This could be the first night of creation.
Beings lie just under the earth's surface, about
to take form. Enormous elbows and skulls press
taut against the hide of grass. No details show.
The smooth glassy sky flattens everything
to silhouettes. Rounded dark shapes
are babies still within their mothers,
lumpy movements under skin.

Only mammals will come into this world,
with long flanks and frizzed surfaces.
Lumbering bears do not quite
arise. Buffalo humps take form,
but they are not yet animals with horns
and brown-agate eyes. Red-tailed hawks
wait for dawn before they appear
on cottonwood trees. Mice and voles
might hide in the thick dry grass

but now nothing is visible as cold wind
blows on a blank, gullied planet.
We can create anything here and forget
when Spanish traders came or Kaw Indians
or sunburned cattle drovers. Soil-waves
ripple the flinty crust as sun transforms horizon
into molten fire, and then—shadows sleep.

These days more bison herds live in Kansas than when I was a child, and these shaggy beasts resemble the land itself. The resurgence of bison makes this century's artifacts seem even more ephemeral. My ancestors arrived here in the 1870s, and this brief history collapses in the Flint Hills, where often telephone poles and gravel roads are the only references to habitation

When I travel, I look for historic underpinnings of a place: the Roman aqueduct stones of Paris rearranged into walls or the schist of the Maine coast. This habit, of looking at origins, comes from living close to the grasslands. The Flint Hills are the largest unplowed tract of virgin prairie on the continent, a fact I took for granted until I became a poet. The sense of the past is palpable. The sense of vertical dimension is like no other. My ultimate, selfish goal is to induce a trance-like state of perception. I want to travel sky country with words.

W. T. P.: Do you identify yourself as a "regional poet"? What power is there in that term?

D. L.: Writings about this part of the country are scarce. I used to feel left out of the New York-based mainstream publishing industry, but now I am more interested in suggesting some ideas about this particular environment for this region's people, now and in the future. I see a lot of disconnection from the land in our culture, and I hope in my writing—whether it is set in Thailand (my most recent book is *Thailand Journal*) or along the Kansas River—to reconnect my own thoughts to the bedrock.

Because I work among American Indian/Alaskan Native people, I have a sense of how young Euro-American cultures are. I am also aware of the thefts, borrowings, and interactions between European and North American indigenous peoples. From this history comes the thin overlay of the present: our malls, pastures, and highways (based on old game trails).

I have heard Ojibway writer Gerald Vizenor speak of how land changes a people. After so many generations and hundreds and thousands of years, the land interacts with people's physical survival and consequently their cultures as well. I feel this subtle impact of land is in beginning stage for English-language people and their literature. I am a small part of this process.

INFLUENCE OF WORKSPACE ON WRITING

WTP: Is there anything about your workspace(s) both past and present that have influenced the ways you write?

DL: I prefer to write in my back yard. Direct contact with elements makes my writing more honest. A limited experience with Zen meditation (I am also a failed Buddhist) helps me to focus attention on immediate surroundings rather than my own contrivances. More than half of my poems begin outdoors. Actual contact with the real, outer world—with its myriad patterns—is my best inspiration, even if the world is glimpsed only through a window.

Right now, indoors, I see the crescent moon through the window, shrouded in a misty corona. A frond of maple leaves breaks the view as well as a paned window and a stiff white-lace curtain. I wear glasses, and I have language and emotional experiences that further distort the view. Though obscured, the moon is nonetheless the most immediate, the most real thing I have seen all day.

I have not been able to write about the moon much. I have one reference to a moon in daylight sky in Moab, Utah: "Above, the ghost moon/ rises through broken sky" ("How to Read Petroglyphs"). I have the goal of writing one good line about the moon. I write in sight of the sun or moon whenever I can, in the hope I can find that one life-changing line. I dream of building a writing studio in my back yard under the pine tree and under the moon. Until then, chairs by windows and outdoor tables are the best places to write. The moon's shifting shapes are within sight.

WRITER AS CHRONICLER

WTP: Are you interested in chronicling places through your poetry, giving them a chance to live on, even though places change?

DL: Yes, I am interested in giving voice to the experiences of my region. My grandmother was a poet, but as a woman, she had no chance to express herself except to a small circle of friends and family. She introduced me to T'Ang dynasty poets and the translations of Kenneth Rexroth. I write in her memory and the memory of all my people who labored to survive with limited personal and public expression. I am from a mixed Appalachian ancestry, and I can only imagine the hardships that drove my forbears from that region.

Historic experience is an obsession. I read the Ezra Pound's *Love Poems of Ancient Egypt* as a teenager, and I was touched by the texture of individual experience at a particular place and time. The lines had immediacy:

Look! a redfish flashed through my fingers!
You'll see it better
If you come over here,
Near me.

The idea that I could follow the word-imprint of some distant person amazed me. I want to preserve aspects of daily life with the same texture, in this time and place, perhaps to inspire some youngster in the future. Perhaps that is a way of returning to my own first inspiration and to my grandmother's tutelage. Focus on the present also helps me keep my bearings in the maelstrom of passing time.

I have lived in the same town mostly since 1967. I feel nurtured by this place, and I write about it when I can, to repay generosity of the people, of the riverwater I drink, and of the land itself. I am a member of the Prairie Writers Circle of The Land Institute, and in that role, I hope to connect narrative with place so that more care is taken with land.

Leslie Marmon Silko's essay "Interior and Exterior Landscapes" describes Laguna Pueblo thought about the unity of humans and land. She breaks down the idea of Cartesian duality: "Rocks and clay are part of the Mother. They emerge in various forms, but at some time before they were smaller particles of great boulders. At a later time they may again become what they once were: dust. A rock shares this fate with us and with animals and plants as well. A rock has being or spirit." The Kansas grasslands and rivers are not a separate "wilderness," but rather the very matter of my bones, flesh, and blood. The opening of my poem "Starwater" expresses this idea:

Nursing my first baby
I drank eight glasses of water,
two quarts, each day. He grew.

I felt like a carrier for water,
passing it on through to the child,
and some day his child, too,
will fatten, remarkable
like peaches and muskmelons
leaching juice from bare dirt.
Astronomers tell us stardust
once swirled together,
cooled into rocks and water
and still circulates,
the same matter pulled into stars
and Earth and into our flesh.

So water travels the skies,
stretches into clouds,
and falls, falling ever East,
circling, the same ancient water
caught in the whirlwind
binding us all together—
gravity, or maybe as we know it
love, or water drawing together
all its kin.

Low, Denise. *New and Selected Poems*. Lawrence: Penthe, 2000.

An Interview Conducted by Karen Hellekson:
On Writing, Regionalism, Women's Issues, American Indian Influences

LEARNING TO WRITE BY EDITING

Karen Hellekson: Let's start with your Cottonwood Review *connection. You were on the staff for five years—in what capacity? How did you feel about* Cottonwood *at that time?*

Denise Low: Editing *Cottonwood* at the University of Kansas is how I got started writing in many ways. I went to my first staff meeting, and Michael Smetzer announced, "I'm getting ready to quit. Is there anyone who would like to be editor?" No one spoke up. Though I was a raw beginner, I stayed after the meeting and said, "I might like to do this." I worked under him and later edited and co-edited, and learned just a great deal from reading the mailings that came in and from writing grants. I tried to get the publication on schedule, tried to up the submissions.

I really learned to see writing in the larger sense of not only the writer-reader relationship, but also everything that goes in between. I think that gives you an appreciation of the whole process.

KH: And you started writing as a result of this experience?

DL: I had been writing off and on. I had written nothing through my BA degree because I could never get into a creative writing class; they were always closed. I did have some good encouragement from a few teachers, including Beth Schultz. I did nothing, of course, during my MA, and then I had two kids. I just started when I took Victor Contoski's class.

He is so gracious never to bring up my early poems! He talks about how important it is to destroy your early work. He's absolutely right.

The other education was working simultaneously, really, with *Cottonwood*. Somehow I decided we should do more books. I edited *Thirty Kansas Poets* and wrote a grant for the Kansas Arts Commission—totally as a beginner, in my twenties, and just going by instinct. I got the grant, a small grant, and everyone said, "Why are you printing 500 copies of that book? No one in Kansas reads poetry." Nonetheless, we went through one printing in six months and then reprinted and went through a second printing. Five years later, we did *Confluence*, an updated Kansas poetry anthology, which I edited again, and it sold out.

DILEMMAS OF REGIONAL WRITING

There really is a need for regional literature. People really do like to read about themselves. The national media just do not represent this milieu accurately or kindly. I think that there is a real discrimination against the Midwest. Wes Jackson writes in *Altars of Hewn Stone* that one reason is the Midwest is what so many people left after the farm economy failed.

KH: It's East and West Coasts; they skip us in between.

DL: Everywhere from jokes on *Cheers* to the *New Yorker*. I don't think there's an understanding of some of the values that form the Midwestern ethic. And not much patience or really any need to learn them, since there are only a few people in Kansas. There are a lot of well-educated Kansans, but they are not involved in high culture, if only because they are far away from each other and have had other priorities in the short history of European-Americans culture in this state. Actually, Kansans do read, more than the national average, according to the book distributors I've talked to, and I think the coasts just don't respond to that market.

KH: Speaking as someone who used to work in a bookstore, our regional section always did extremely well. But look at popular items: anything about Jesse James sold well. Cookbooks.

DL: New York City is a wonderful place, but it is a region. Many publishers happen to be in that region, and they want to read about their own region. I have a friend, a professional writer, with an agent and publications, who wrote a novel set in Omaha. Literally, her agent read the first draft and said, "My dear, you must make this more upscale and move it to New York." That's where the agent's population center is, where her sense of the market is. But in the meantime, where does that leave the Midwest? This exact thing has happened to several other people I know.

KH: Southern writers get a lot of attention also. I think it's time for the Midwest to come to the fore. But it will take writers to start writing about it and then hit it big.

DL: And find publishers and distributors for it. I wonder if this attitude—that settings in literature are interchangeable—has a connection to capitalist exploitation of the land. In my own writing, I feel an obligation to the hills and rivers that support my life, to elaborate on their place in human culture.

KH: Setting is an important part of anything you write. Suddenly switching it to the East Coast—

DL: Well, that changes it completely. So you have a Midwesterner, with that sensibility, writing a novel set in New York. It's still going to have Midwestern sensibilities spliced onto a different place. Anyway, it's confusing because it's really hard to pin down what the Midwestern voice is. And a lot of Midwesterners migrate to New York and the West Coast.

KH: Do you see yourself as part of the Midwestern voice?

DL: Sure. This is where I grew up, and this is the place I know. I have trouble sometimes with people from other parts of the country, communicating, because they take a Midwestern reticence for blandness. William Stafford belies misconceptions about Midwesterners, a perfect example. And as a woman, I go through all of that passive stereotyping due to gender, and further, as a Midwesterner, I was taught not to be too flamboyant or be the center of attention and not to stand out and not to hog the conversation. I think some people misinterpret that as not having anything to say. I've just had a number of interesting encounters through the years where people have thought I was really stupid. I finally figured out what was going on and learned to shift into another kind of dialect in talking to these people.

KH: A lot of it might be politeness too. I'm from Minneapolis, Minnesota, where guilt is ingrained in you. Even now, I'll feel incredible guilt about things. There's no way around it; I just have to deal with it, but it can be an amazing stumbling block. If other people don't feel that, you can't use your traditional strategies to manipulate them in ways that you're used to. Strategies that work in Minneapolis won't work in, say, New York. It's weird.

70

DL: If the other person isn't a part of that paradigm, then you're totally out of the circle. It's an interesting thing, and also within the Midwest, you're not taken as seriously as a writer. My parents have been very good about being as supportive as well as they could, but of course, my parents say, "Can't you write anything but poetry?"

KH: *A bodice-ripper or something that will sell!*

DL: Exactly. It's not a writer's community in some of the smaller towns of Kansas. These are reader communities. I go out for the Kansas Council for Humanities programs and speak in some of these small-town libraries. But the audience wants to read what's new in New York. I think there's a real sense of inferiority that's not accurate, but that people out in the tiny towns of Kansas have. Because they are isolated, they feel they are not up to or equal to the Coasts. In fact, one of the best audiences I have had was a Leavenworth, Kansas, women's book group. It was traditional women who were meeting in the afternoon. These women had read everything on the *New York Times* bestseller list as well recent literary fiction. They had the most insightful questions and educated comments about my writing of any audience I've seen.

JOURNALS, MEMORY, AND POETRY

KH: *Let's turn to your poetry. I'm struck by your use of memory, of reliving events, of wanting to stretch out experience. How does your poetry capture memory, distill it?*

DL: Those are very good observations because one of my goals is to live my life as fully as possible. Writing for me really does stretch out time. It defines it, it preserves it, and it gives it more dimensions. I'm fascinated by time and memory and what you remember and what you choose not to remember, which is the focus of "Selective Amnesia," published in *Stiletto*. I had some experiences as a child that I blocked out and then those memories did come back as an adult. I also have a very good memory: I remember things from when I was a little baby in a cradle. I have a lot of distinct memories from when I was a tiny child.

KH: *You also keep journals, judging by some of the entries in your essay in* Tulip Elegies. *Does that help stretch out memory also?*

DL: Yes. It's fascinating to see how different I am from the journal writer of five years ago, say. I ran across one of the first poems I wrote that hadn't been destroyed. I was such a different person, yet I was the same person, and these shifts are all the identity of Denise Low.

KH: I never keep a journal, but I did when I was in England, because I thought I might want to remember my half-year there. Even now, when I read it—and I don't often do that—I suddenly remember things I had completely forgotten about. It serves as a jog for my memory. I relive experiences in a really intimate, almost physical way. Does that happen to you too?

DL: Oh, yes. In fact, this is crazy, but I just had a tooth refilled this week. As the dentist removed it, through the layers—that one filling has been redone like three different times—I went through the layers of remembering all the way back to my very first dentist. It was very physical. It brought back this crusty old Kansas dentist who had the slowest drill in the West.

INFLUENCE OF AMERICAN INDIAN PHILOSOPHIES

KH: Let's bring the topic back around to Native Americans. Of course, you teach at Haskell Indian Nations University. The Native American influence on your work is unmistakable. Can you speak a bit on the impact of Indians on your life experience, poetry?

DL: That's a really complicated question! I hope there's an influence, and I've been wondering what it is. I grew up in southern Kansas, in Emporia, and there were a number of people of Indian ancestry around me, some of whom were very influential. One of my writing projects is to get in touch with an old high school friend and write about a man who mentored both of us at a certain point in our lives who was Cherokee. These people around Emporia then didn't have the real reservation experience; they didn't have the continuity of their traditions; but they had something. Towards the end of my years in Emporia, a man who had been my father's best friend came to acknowledge his Indian ancestry and his ties with it. The man, Jack LeClair Haggard, an Ojibway, started powwows in Emporia then, in the 1970s.

Certainly I am of mostly Northern European background, but there were a lot of Indian people whom I knew as a child. In Emporia, there just were a lot of Indians: neighbors and teachers. It wasn't a big thing; it was just like you're part Irish or you're a part Cherokee or part Chippewa. Of course, I was ignorant of the destructive influence of Indian boarding schools; I was ignorant of what was really going on. Nevertheless, I wonder about indirect interaction between the cultures and maybe that has influenced me. I started reading Mari Sandoz when I was eight or nine. I've always seen Native American history as a crucial part of the history of this region.

KH: When I go to Indian art shows—Haskell Indian College has one every year, and of course they have them in Minnesota at powwows and related events—it seems that the artwork is concerned with the Indians' past, not with what is going on now. Instead of a focus on what's here and now, there's an idealized past. Do you think that's a problem?

DL: I think that's an accurate perception. When I teach creative writing at Haskell, I try very hard to get my students to look at the whole picture and not to buy into clichés. Also, part of the problem is there are non-Indians who want to buy clichés from the past. They perpetuate that market. In another form, *Dances With Wolves* is a similar example.

KH: How does your own work fit into that? Your poetry mostly focuses, again, on the past, not the present.

DL: Each poem has a dialectic of past and present. I really do believe that memory is power, and conscious awareness of the past informs the present. I do want to create poetry that has an impact on the present moment, and I think to get depth, which is really important to me, that you do have to go through layers of past experience.

KH: The Native American influence seems tied in to your sense of place. You mention the Ogallala Aquifer, as well as the Midwest in general and Kansas in particular. Place seems to pin down, solidify, experience—even the earth itself. What is your connection to place?

DL: I'm very conscious, and have been since I was very small, that there is a history with this land—of people, of rocks, of animals. In *Spring Geese*, I spend a lot of time with fossils—getting down to the bedrock. I just think it's important for a culture to be informed of where it has come from in order to make intelligent decisions and expressions of its present and future. I think a poet's job is to digest and synthesize as much as possible in order to give voice to community experience, including history. I think this is part of an ecological consciousness, the most crucial politics now.

KH: I'm curious about the use of religion in your poetry. Sometimes you adopt a Jewish persona ("Pray for the People"), sometimes a Christian one, sometimes neither, as in "Easter Morning," where a couple celebrates Easter not by going to church but by making love. Where does religion fit in?

DL: That's an interesting question, and it ties in to my attraction to Native American literature that I read. Native American literature allows for spirituality, whereas in contemporary European-American literature, if you write from a Christian point of view, it's discarded as naive or sentimental. In popular fiction especially, you read nothing that's religious in a conscious way. I can only think of a few books: *The Handmaid's Tale*, by Margaret Atwood, a Canadian, which is an interesting take on fundamentalism.

KH: Philippe Sollers' Women.

DL: Yes, in places—coming to terms with Catholicism. And I think it is to Sollers' credit that he is thinking about it. In a lecture at Berkeley, I heard Paula Gunn Allen, a Laguna Pueblo writer, point out the implicit influence of Puritanism on Americans, even on people who never set foot in a church. Values and worldview are passed on. But it is interesting—the selective amnesia that the academic writing culture has: Thou Shalt Not Write About Christianity or conventional religion, although Zen is okay; it's more hip. I really do want my work to have spiritual content—whatever that mystery is exactly. I don't strive for an orthodox Christian set of symbols.

But take alchemy. I've studied the symbology of astrology since I was sixteen. There really are some wonderful metaphors for the whole life process that come out of the European alchemical and astrological traditions, and out of Christian mysticism. I really would like to be able to evoke some of those levels in a way that is powerful to people. I like the work of Michael Hefferman, who uses Catholic angels and saints. It's a richer set of cultural artifacts than the Congregational Church's Protestantism in my background.

WOMEN'S ISSUES

KH: I know feminist concerns are of special interest to you. How and where does feminism intersect with your work, your beliefs? Do you see your writing as a feminist expression?

DL: I am a woman; I have had a woman's experience. Some of those experiences as a writer have been those of limitation. I've thought about this a lot. I feel I have been dismissed sometimes, and that some of my subjects have been dismissed. I did some early writing on quilting, and gardening is a family tradition. But for many years, as you know, women's culture has been devalued, whereas the guys can get together and write their baseball and bar poems, and that's serious. But a woman writes about her garden—! I had a man say to me, "You're calling this set of poems *Tulip Elegies*? Isn't that kind of flip?" For me, [tulips are] incredibly sensual, rich, evocative objects.

I try to be respectful of male culture. Still, I am aware in numerous instances of being belittled for being a woman, and I conclude that a technique of that belittlement has been harassment, since I was a small. Speaking is a kind of basic power, like writing, and when men, especially men who are teachers, shift their attention from a woman's words to her body, they sabotage her sense of comfortable power in the world. I think my experience as a Midwestern woman is not atypical. The women I have talked to have been through much of the same harassment. I think it's important for me to speak about it.

KH: *How are—or were—you able to assert your voice in such an environment?*

DL: Several things. I have a very wonderful older brother, and he was very good to me when I was a little kid—six years older. He always made me feel like a dignified human being. When he came back from Harvard in the summers, he would give me writing assignments and encourage me to be a writer.

I have been fortunate through all of this to have had men as mentors—and of course all my publishers have been men. I really like men, and I think having had a really good relationship with my brother, I feel very comfortable with men who are treating me in a respectful manner. I've had very good mentoring at different points from Jim Bogan, Vic Contoski, Steven Meats down at Pittsburg State, who helped me at a certain stage of my writing that led to *Starwater*, and I'm very grateful to him and to the many men who are colleagues and friends and editors and publishers—Michael Annis, Dan Jaffee, George Wedge, and James Gilkeson.

KH: *And have you formed connections with women as well?*

DL: Yes, I like women too. But look at the women editors and publishers in the Midwest—who are they? I'm on the board of Woodley Press at Washburn University, which specifically has guidelines to publish writing from Kansas, or writing with some connection to Kansas. Of the twenty-some books published by Woodley over the years, only two are by women. There just aren't many Midwestern women who make it through to be writers and publishers. Name me a woman publisher besides Gloria Vando in the entire area. And she's from New York—a Puerto Rican from New York.

KH: I think her presence might still encourage women.

DL: Oh, yes. She's worked very hard for women's writing, through *Helicon Nine*.

KH: I think it will also help that women's concerns are being taken much more seriously. On the academic front, feminist criticism is becoming more important.

DL: You see that through the academic side; my focus more is on creative writers in the Midwest.

KH: For example, you mentioned quilting. That seems to have become lately the big metaphor for women's concerns—for coming together and creating something. The AIDS quilt in some ways comes out of that whole idea. Some of the icons that used to be laughed at are now being taken much more seriously by everyone. Do you see feminism as affecting your work in any way? How does it affect what you write?

DL: It encourages me. I see myself writing as a person rather than sitting down as a woman, or as a Midwestern woman.

KH: So you write from human experience.

DL: Right. I really am not thinking of the ideology of anything. I want most of all to be known as a writer and not as a poetess.

KH: With the condescending little -ess on the end!

THEMES OF MORTALITY IN POETRY: *TULIP ELEGIES*

KH: Let's turn to Tulip Elegies, *your latest book of poetry, just out from Penthe Press. The essay comprising the second half of your most recent work,* Tulip Elegies, *seems intensely personal—more so, perhaps, than the poems themselves. I know* Tulip Elegies *was written as a response to your father's stroke. But you also mention the death of Cecil Dawes, Junior, a Haskell student who disappeared and was later found dead in the Kaw River. How does that death fit into the poems? I think your father's stroke is fairly self-evident, but how does this other concern, which happened at the same time, become involved with this work?*

DL: It was a series of events that happened to me in my mid-30s, when I experienced death and divorce. I really did not have a language or imagination that included those things. I had a much more static sense of things: you grow up, you get married, you sort things out in a certain way, and you stay that way. There is a happily-ever-after that all of our movies end with: the couple gets together after a long courtship, and that's the end. The basic verb of English, "to be," implies a static state. This was shattered by the tragic shooting death of my son's best friend when my son was thirteen. It began a series of disintegrations for me.

I had known Cecil Dawes, Junior, at Haskell, had worked with his father, and when he died, that just brought up again the horrible tragedy of losing children. You lose not just the person but that person's entire future, all those years that would have stretched before him. Cecil's death stirred up that loss of [another friend], a thirteen-year-old boy. He had been very close to my family, a very close playmate and companion, and in the house a lot. Losing Cecil—again, it's losing a part of myself. Wanting to come to terms with all of that is what led to the poems.

KH: At the very end of Tulip Elegies, *there are a couple lines that the Dawes family adopted a child after Cecil's death. I was wondering if that tied into the whole concept of renewal that seems to be implicit in* Tulip Elegies.

DL: Definitely. I was very conscious of it. The Dawes' adoption of a baby is an act of hope. We have to accept with the gift of life that also loss is a gift. The fact that we do come to an end gives life its characteristics.

KH: Could you speak also on your father's stroke? There's a beautiful essay about it in Tulip Elegies.

DL: At that difficult time, I gave myself permission to start writing about it. The publisher, Jim Gilkeson, said to me, "This is such a striking set of poems. Is there anything more? Can you explain the process of how it got written?" I'm very grateful to Jim Gilkeson for prompting me to write about that. It really helped me a great deal to take all of this and pull it together.

My father had a stroke in August of 1989. I had just returned from a summer in California, when I got a call from my mother. I knew my life had just changed. It really is a shock to see a powerful, articulate, strong-willed person undergo this kind of change. He was a very talkative man, and he still cannot speak. Losing speech is a horrible change for people. It cuts you off from so much. He also cannot read.

KH: It would be amazingly frustrating: to be able to think completely coherently without being able to express oneself.

DL: It's just sort of a Kafka-esque metamorphosis that was so quick. It was a very sudden thing. One day he's playing golf; that night he's in a hospital and can only blink.

CONCLUSION

KH: The last question: What are you working on next? I assume you're already working.

DL: Of course, of course, it's always in process. In 1991 I was very grateful to win the Kansas Arts Commission Literary Arts Fellowship in poetry, which they give once every three years to one poet. This tells you about the level of funding for the arts for this state. To acknowledge my appreciation, I started a set of poems and prose pieces about the Midwest and this area, about Kansas. I'm trying to write very honestly and accurately about an individual experience that I hope belies the stereotypes that the coastal media present as Kansas.

KH: So you're going to spread the true message!

DL: Well—yes. But there are some people that say you should keep it a dark secret, that living this marginalized existence has its own advantages, which it does. You don't get into the academic games; you don't get too comfortable. There are some real advantages. So maybe it should be kept a secret. Let people stay away.

Notes on the poem "Elegy for July 28, 1994

I use writing to focus my mind on the world around me. My own experience is forty-five years of living in Kansas, as a descendant of other Kansans. I do not set out to write about this particular place, but because of my commitment to writing as dialogue, not monologue, I explore what is around me; therefore, images of this region appear in my work. I am interested in how objects and places, such as the crooked pine tree on the road to Stull, accumulate cultural and personal associations. I owe to Elizabeth Schultz, a professor at the University of Kansas, my interest in how people complicate objects around them with histories, memories, and literature.

Each spring when the Waneta plum tree in my back yard blooms, I see a Japanese fruit tree growing in Kansas soil. I also see "Petals on a wet, black bough." I hope to add such complications to the regional landscape when I write about it. I also hope to show the complexity of the Midwestern state where I reside.

What is around me is not the bleak, gray world of *The Wizard of Oz*, but a shapeshifting ocean of towns and sky and people and roadways. Always when I write, I return to William Carlos Williams' precept, "No ideas but in things." I try to elaborate on the plains of Kansas—the time and place where I write. I cannot help, then, but write in the voice I learned as I grew up at the edge of the Flint Hills. I have lived no other place.

Elegy for July 28, 1994

Cicadas ratchet against air
as sun withdraws from
the garden leaf by leaf.

Dark collects around
the first fireflies.

Sycamore leaves lie still—
limp banners against trunks
of the neighbor's trees.

Downtown the Gods of this day
lean against a wall

with the old men and talk
until the last light and then
dissolve into stonework

faces flattening, disappearing
as though they never existed.

Notes for *Learning the Language of Rivers*

In a recent lecture, Kurt Vonnegut stated that reading is Western-style meditation. I find writing also to be meditative, and a process of discovery. While writing a long historical poem last fall, I counted back generations and realized that I am a fifth generation Kansan (and I am the only one in my family in this generation still residing in Kansas). I write many different kinds of things—book reviews, some articles, short stories—but I engage in writing poetry in a more passionate way. I am compelled by the concentration of energy in a poem.

During my high school years, my brother, David Dotson, and my sister, Jane Ciabattari, encouraged me to write as did some fine teachers, including Marjorie Sullivan. I started as a student at the University of Kansas with the intention of studying creative writing or classics. The creative writing classes were always closed because of over-enrollment, so I majored in ancient history and then English. Elizabeth Schultz of the English Department was encouraging, but I quit writing poetry throughout the time I was earning my B.A. and M.A. degrees. I did see many fine poets during that time, however, including Ed Dorn, Robert Bly, and Robert Kelly. I also married and had two children.

After graduation I taught English part-time at Kansas State University and then at K.U. In 1978 I became a reader for *Cottonwood Review*, and in 1979 I took some poetry writing classes from Victor Contoski. I was encouraged by a number of other friends at that time, including Jim Bogan, Don Byrd, and Robert Greene. In the early 1980s I commuted to Wichita State and earned an M.F.A. in poetry.

Sunsets have been a strong influence on my poetry. While growing up in Emporia, I often sat on our fort porch and felt the different colors of the sunset filtering through the air. I read Rudolf Steiner and C.W. Leadbeater about color, but mostly I associate the dramatic shift from daylight to dark with poetry by Li Po and Tu Fu (given to me by my grandmother, who was a poet), and with some of the early beat poetry. Somehow in junior high, in the mid-sixties, I got hold of an anthology of beat poets, including Gary Snyder, Allen Ginsberg, Diane DiPrima, and Jack Micheline. Their energy in words came very close to duplicating the intensity I felt in sunsets, snowstorms, wind, and spring bulbs—the thrust of natural cycles within a prairie town.

Interview with a Kansas Author by Linda Jones McCoy:
Prairie and American Indian Influences, Business of Writing and Teachers.

PRAIRIE INFLUENCES

Linda Jones McCoy: You talk in Touching the Sky *about your grandmother, your mother, your hometown, and the Flint Hills. Just what influence did those people and that setting have on your growing up? In other words, what was your early life like?*

Denise Low: That's always a tough question because I have nothing else to compare it to. It's the only growing up I know. I now recognize, after traveling and after being an adult looking back, that it really was a unique experience. This is a very young culture on the plains. This was less than seven generation s from Wounded Knee, which was the end of the Indian wars. In the 1950s, the Flint Hills range was still used for grazing—cattle instead of buffalo. It was a transition time from the way it had been used through thousands of years by American Indians up to the cultural changes of European Americans. So now I look back and see how this region preserved a way of life that does have roots back tens of thousands of years. The burning of prairies, for example, is something that European Americans took from the example of American Indian friends and relatives and continued. There are cattle instead of buffalo and many other species, but still, it really is a kind of unique corner of the world.

LJM: And quiet for the most part, even though you were in town.

DL: Yes, it was quiet. Of course at the time I chafed, and I wished I were somewhere more romantic. I got letters from my oldest sister, who moved to California, and all that sounded wonderful. And I tried to move to California to go to graduate school, but that fell through, and I found myself back here.

LJM: Did that setting, you think, influence the way you feel about people and places today?

DL: Oh, very much so. I think that where you grow up sets your spatial thermostat or how you think of space, the personal space you expect around yourself. I think of a lot of obvious and subtle ways that this sets how you interact with the world. Now my nervous system is not structured to large cities like Kansas City or New York. Every time I go to the city, I enjoy it, and then I want to get out. I get over stimulated very quickly. And I have to be in an urban environment a long time to begin to dull myself enough to put up shields between myself and so many other people.

LJM: Is Lawrence too big of a town?

DL: Almost. It's getting there. It's really changed in the last five years. And I'm having some problems with that.

W RITING P ROCESS

LJM: What is your daily routine like now? I'm thinking here about how you juggle your time with your family, your friends, and your students?

DL: My day is very filled. And I guess I've always worked that way. I do try to find time every day to be outdoors in the backyard to slow down, look at the sky a minute or something like that, or the phase of the moon. I do try to calm myself in that fashion, but I teach twelve credit hours at Haskell. I have advisees, I have writings that I do for the department, and also I do a lot of critical writing in Native American Literature. I have reviews that are assigned to me. I have a lot of deadlines. I keep my list on a day calendar. I manage to get through a couple of days of not too much going on, but I have to try to not be pressured.

LJM: Do you have a block of time every day you try and write, or do you catch it when you can catch it? Do you set yourself a goal for a certain number of pages a day, anything along that line?

DL: I think every person has a way of writing. I find for myself, I go in phases where I am writing a lot, and then I lie fallow a lot. And I've

84

learned to be patient with the fallow times, and mostly those times are when I don't have enough time. You know, my mother is widowed and I have responsibilities with her. My family life is important to me. And my sons spend a lot of time at home too. So weekly I do try to get about five pages of personal writing done.

LJM: What are the tools that you use? I see two computers sitting here in your office and a typewriter on your shelf and paper and pencils and so on.

DL: I use everything. I used to only compose by long hand, and I long for those days because there was something very satisfying about that muscular expenditure of energy coordinating with the subconscious and the conscious minds in the act of writing. And these days I just don't have time for that. I do a lot of composing, even some poetry, on the computer, and the computer is just a wonderful tool.

LJM: Would you say you're a disciplined writer or do you write in spurts?

DL: Spurts, like my life is in spurts. I sort of prioritize, and one of my priorities has been not writing but rather house painting. I've been painting my house, and for me that's a very satisfying physical balance to my life. I sit at a desk too much. I really try to live a conscious, balanced life as much as I can. So that was a discipline, and I think I stuck to it. I don't know whether you would call it disciplined or obsessive compulsive. I just sort of stayed with it, until I finished it. I do like the sense of finishing, and the sense of accomplishment I get, whether it's from painting the house or seeing a new book off the press

LJM: How much do you write in your head before you sit down?

DL: There's a significant intuitive flicker in my head, and there's a certain degree of intensity to an idea that's a visual, intellectual, and emotional impulse all at once. And when that comes, I know I should follow it. This is after many years of learning to recognize my own process.

Today, for example, after four or five days of very pure, clear weather, I noticed the clouds come in. I had this sense of the clouds being like a ceiling of a room. The clouds are quite interesting after all that clarity. So a lot of things started to accumulate about the complexities that arise out of a whole set of clouds that I've never seen before. And I realize I'm working on a manuscript called *A Daybook of Interiors*, where I'm really trying to describe the nests that we build for ourselves both physically and psychologically. To me that push in my mind to look at the sky as a ceiling, to look at the complexities of this particular ceiling, I know that I need to get that written down, and I jotted down a few notes before you came.

LJM: Do you ever wake in the middle of the night and jot notes?

DL: Never. Never. Sleep is sacred.

Differences between Poetry and Prose

LJM: I would say for the person who rarely or never writes poetry, poetry would seem very different form writing prose. Since you do both of them, does it seem very different to you?

DL: Yes, it does. As I said, I write a number of critical articles and critical reviews that go in academic journals, and I use the journalistic side of my brain. I know we are supposed to have left and right sides, but I don't. Instead, I have the lyrical side and the documentary side. I am grateful for a good education and a lot of experiences and opportunities in writing, because I have learned how to write journalistically. I wrote a high school column for the *Emporia Gazette* for two years when I was a teenager. I think pretty quickly, and that is the trick to journalistic writing—get it ripped off as expeditiously as you can. And then the other side is the pleasure, the lyrical side. I have an MFA in creative writing. I've been able to work with some of the best writers and learn from them. And I really think there are some tendencies when you train in academic creative writing programs to be removed from the gutsy realities of life. Nonetheless, I value those academic experiences very much because I feel they have shortened the time it has taken me to learn how to write.

LJM: You have flow maybe?

DL: Well, you just learn more quickly what is good writing and what is bad writing.

LJM: Is journalism spare writing and is poetry spare writing?

DL: I think that journalism is one-dimensional writing, and I think that poetry is multi-dimensional.

LJM: Good answer. That is very interesting.

DL: Journalistic is "what you see is what you get." Who, what, when, where, why? And in poetry, each sentence is loaded. Each poem, I hope, is evocative.

LJM: I think that most if not all poets, and I include you in that group, seem to have a deeper sense of the importance of relationships both with people and with nature than other people do. Do you agree with that?

DL: I agree with that. I think there's a particular turn of mind that I have, and I recognize in a number of people, including my husband Tom Weso, very strongly the tendency to look at the overview, to see the networks of inter-relationships. Maybe this kind of mentality does not as easily remember factual details. I think there are emphases in the sites of the brain. I think the part in my brain that is more developed is the one that sees connections. I cannot remember strings of numbers, though.

LJM: Are you tender-hearted?

DL: Oh, only if I have to be. [Laughter.]

LJM: Do you think poets are more tender-hearted than regular folk?

DL: I'd like to think that I'm reasonably sensitive, but I also am very competitive and have a lot of drive. I don't know if that's because it's hard to maintain an involvement in the fine arts, especially in writing, in this day and age. I feel there's a certain toughness you need to survive.

I remember George Gurley and I were commuting to teach at Washburn University in the 1980s, and he and I were the two poets on the staff at that time, although we were teaching composition. We would go into department meetings, and he and I were the ones who were insisting that our students learn grammar. And others were saying, "Oh, well, we want them to explore and feel personally involved with what they're writing," and so forth. And he and I were both the only ones who would hold out for "This is a discipline; this is something they're going to need; this is a utilitarian obligation we have here."

LJM: I read once that—I don't know if the author was black or white—she was a teacher who often met with black teachers, and the black teachers would beg her to teach them grammar because they said that every teacher they had come to would say, "Oh, you already know it," or "Your language is acceptable," and so on. And they said, "If you know something that we don't know, would you please tell us." And it seems what you're saying here is let them in on the secret of what the language structure is. Don't hold it from them.

DL: Yes, And I think that even though we think of the grammar as something very rote, the real mystery of being human is locked in the language. This really is one of the things we have that makes us different from other species, and it really is very mysterious how this works. A disciplined study of language, I think, is a meditative path as much as any other.

LJM: I think that leads me into a question. In Touching the Sky *you don't mention teachers much, either public school or university. Was there a teacher somewhere who taught you how to write or who at least encouraged you to write?*

DL: Oh, absolutely. I really did bond at young ages with my teachers. I always adored my teachers, even the scary ones. And I think that identification was important. I remember being in grade school, and I thought to myself each year, "I want to be a teacher," and each year it would be the grade I was at. So probably by the time I'm in college, I thought even then, I would want to teach at the college level. I remember that early. And I was fortunate to go to a school at a time where the education that was routinely served out was very good. I had some remarkable teachers, women mostly, who mentored me and gave me books to read and encouraged me. Dale Keller and Jim Williams, who are now at Hutchinson Community College and Johnson County Community College, respectively, were two male mentors.

I could talk at length about the difficulties of being a woman from my background and being a writer. I think it was not an easy generation or time or place to do that. I think Midwestern women are encouraged to be quiet, tend the house, and so forth—at least at that time. But still, I had a great deal of encouragement in college and later on from men who were writers and very respectful, in appropriate relationships.

LJM: I have some fun books on teaching children how to write poetry, particularly Kenneth Koch's Wishes, Lies and Dreams *and Myra Cohn Livingston has a book called* Poem Making: Ways to Begin Writing Poetry, *and they show in both of those books how you can introduce various patterns of poetry even to very young children. I'm interested in how you learned to write poetry. Did someone introduce you to poetry forms and actually teach you how to write poetry that way?*

DL: Certainly. I think we are introduced to structure and language through a number of ways: songs, rhymes, when we're very little kids. I remember in fourth grade officially being given an assignment to write a poem and feeling empowered and proud of myself for that.

LJM: Was it built around any particular form?

DL: Rhyme schemes.

LJM: Just rhymes, then?

DL: Yes. I will say that I felt that instruction in poetry then and today really falls down in the older grades, in secondary school. I did have a few teachers, Lois Jacquith and Marjorie Sullivan, in addition to Williams and Keller, who showed me contemporary poetry. And I started reading beatnik poets in junior high, and this was just really interesting and exciting to me, but the textbooks too often have humorous verses or they don't show that poetry is a way of expressing a wide range of emotions, especially for adolescents.

LJM: I think that comes from research that says that's what children like. Children like poetry that is funny and if you don't give them that they don't tend to like it. So that's probably why the textbooks are like that.

DL: Well, yes up to maybe 11 or 12, but after that I think a wide range of things is appropriate. *A Gift of a Watermelon Pickle* is the name of an anthology that had a William Stafford poem in it that I read over and over when I was in high school. Mrs. Jacquith had it in her room. It wasn't a regular textbook, but she had it sitting around her classroom and encouraged me to read it and made over it like it was exciting. I think as a kid I picked up her enthusiasm as much as anything, but it showed me there was a wider range than what we saw in the textbooks.

LJM: I think what I'm hearing is maybe if you were taught a pattern, this tended to be rhyme the end lines and the rest of what you learned about various patterns of poetry came from reading rather than from instruction.

DL: Oh, absolutely. And I learned as much about the form of poetry from music lessons, learning to present a musical phrase, as from anything else.

THE BUSINESS OF WRITING

LJM: You have published academic analysis as well as creative work. How does each of these fit into your sense of yourself as a writer?

DL: I think of myself as a curious person. I want to know about things. I want to keep learning. I want to keep being a student, and I want to live fully. I don't want to sleepwalk through my life, and so the writing for me in the different modes helps me to achieve my personal goal of being self-aware. The different modes are different aspects of human intelligence and abilities.

LJM: Again, those two sides of your brain that you were talking abut ear-lier. It is quite a problem trying to find ordering information for your poetry books. Are there other problems working with small press publications?

DL: Well, it's hard to find publishers of poetry, period. And I publish with small presses because they will commit themselves to literary pub-lishing, whereas in New York, the publishers, in case anyone's noticed, have gone to corporations and bottom-line publishing. And more and more they're going to blockbuster publishing, and some of this is starting to backfire on them as they publish bad books with a lot of promotion.

The whole publishing business is really in an odd situation right now. It has become very decentralized, and it is hard to get ahold of things outside your region. Most of my books have sold out. They are no longer in print, and Cottonwood Press, with whom I've published several books and anthologies, almost has gone out of existence at this point. And part of this is the budget cuts in the state, other circumstances. So with pub-lishing poetry, it doesn't sell well, so you are left with university presses. In Kansas, our university press will not publish poetry.

LJM: Not at all?

DL: Not at all. The only press that will publish poetry occasionally is Woodley at Washburn University, which will publish one or two titles a year, and since I sit on that board, I hesitate to publish with them. So that means I must compete [for publication] with other [regions'] university presses. That just takes a tremendous amount of energy, which I don't have right now.

I got involved with Jim Gilkeson of Penthe Press, and he came to me and really nurtured my writing. I had a set of poems called "Tulip Ele-gies," and he was very good about working with me and letting me have a personal involvement. I had another manuscript that three presses said they would print and then backed off, broke their word for various rea-sons. Someone got a divorce and moved, someone else moved and went broke, or had other projects come up. It's just difficult. It's a very difficult climate in which to publish, promote, and distribute, and part of this is the distribution, which is really a brutal business.

Barnes and Noble picked up *Touching the Sky*, which is great, or sounds great. Well, they take 55%, and so that leaves the publisher with cost plus mailing expenses, and Barnes and Noble retains the right to return books. After a book's been knocked around and returned, usually it's not resalable and that's a loss. Then by the time you count all those expenses, you break even. And I think my publisher said that he was not quite breaking even with what went out with Barnes and Noble. Yes, it's a difficult, expensive business.

LJM: *The money angle runs the show.*

DL: It does, sure it does. You can subsidize. You can self publish. We used to have grants, and the grants are getting scarce. We used to have university support, and the university's funding has been cut. I respect Fred Woodward at University Press of Kansas, for keeping that press fiscally sound, but the way he's done that is he's cut out anything that is any risk at all, including fiction and poetry. So it's all about business.

LJM: *If you self-publish, is there stigma to that because people call it vanity press?*

DL: Sure there is.

LJM: *So if you don't go with a legit, so to speak, press, then you face that problem.*

DL: Right. Then you get into [questions like] is my work good? Is it not good? Should I be able to go into Atheneum, Wesleyan? But that kind of press, traditional publishers of poetry, have gone under. In the last few years, we've really lost that network. At the same time, more and more people are writing poetry. That's the great irony. I'm not sure they are all reading poetry. I'm not sure they are buying poetry.

LJM: *How are they sharing it then?*

DL: Well, there are all these open mics and poetry slams and so forth that are fun. I mean, I like to see these things. The use of language leads you, whether you plan it or not, to more understanding. I think the study of language is a positive influence on people in many ways—overt and covert. Many times people want to be heard. They want attention, or they want to be discovered or they want to be seen as talented. There's an odd ego thing that goes along with being a writer, being a poet, and people are involved with that rather than also seeing it as one side to a dialogue between reading and writing, giving and receiving.

I think one of the things that I certainly took a long time to figure out as a youngster was that I just wanted to be praised and told how great my writing was. I had one mentor, who would say, "Well, great. Have you read the work of Emily Dickinson?" And I'd be taken aback. I'd say, "Well, why don't you just read my work and take it on its own terms?" I did not understand that if I write a spare, lean line, I should be able to look at Dickinson to see how a master handles the spare, lean line. And it took me a long time to understand about reading being important, using other writers as models, and not feeling that anything I would attempt after Dickinson would be futile.

LJM: You know, where poetry is published is poetry for children, and not by a lot of people. By a very few people, but those few people—I'm thinking of Jack Prelutsky, for example, and Shel Silverstein—are very, very popular. Their books sell, and they've sold for years. They do not go out of print.

AMERICAN INDIAN INFLUENCES ON WRITING
LJM: I take it you have no Indian heritage.

DL: None to speak of.

LJM: I don't know how I can relate this to your writings that makes sense in this interview, but in this setting at Haskell Indian Nations University, surely having been here over the years, you have become very accepted even though sometimes Caucasians are not. Does that relationship with this particular piece of our total culture work itself into your writings in some way?

DL: Of course. Of course it does. Several things happen being immersed, really, in a different culture. One is I have defined my own culture more precisely than, I think, the average person. And I've come to accept the old struggles with the things that are my inheritance and my traditions.

At the same time, I think I have been influenced by the ethnicities of Native American cultures from childhood. In Emporia, Kansas, where I grew up, there were many, many people who were friends of the family, and that I was friends with, who were of some American Indian heritage. And even when it was just a fourth ancestry, I think there is a way of looking at things that has been an interchange on these prairies since the burning of the prairie was taught to European American ranchers by Osage and Kansas Indian people. William Stafford told me he had some Indian ancestry, as well as other artists and writers like Philip Kimball and Stan Herd. I have a fraction. So I don't see my work here at Haskell as isolated from my culture; I see it as a continuum of American Plains culture. And I think there's been great deal of Indian influence on American European culture for hundreds of years. We think of it as going the other way, but I think American Indians have influenced European Americans tremendously, but it just hasn't been acknowledged consciously. Jack Weatherford, in his books like *Indian Givers,* discusses this.

So sure, Native American cultures have influenced my writing. They've influenced my life, and I have been able to trace some of that influence from childhood. I also remain puritanical and European in many, many ways.

LJM: I see the nature connection there, particularly toward the end of Touching the Sky, *and you're talking about the medicine wheel here at Haskell. But you also talk about your garden and that type of thing. So you have that small town Kansas sense as well. We grow a garden and we take care of our fields and so on. But then also the great importance of nature to the American Indian is part of their religion. Is that a correct thing to say?*

DL: Well, I would not say that it is specific to American Indians. I think that the calendar of the church is based on the seasons. I would say that Wordsworth wrote about nature. Nature is not an invention of the American Indians. I think maybe some of them are closer to subsistence existence, and I say that with respect. I have students who come from Alaska and some other states, even Oklahoma and Wisconsin, where hunting is part of the way you get food. They are closer in experience to that, maybe. Yes, I look at the attitude in Genesis towards nature as wilderness rather than as a friend.

Vine DeLoria, Jr., writes about Native American religions being focused on a particular geographic spot where these people live or where urban Indians go back to visit, so that the geography still has the mystery of a sacred place. But my inherited religion took place thousands of miles away, thousands of years ago. And Deloria makes a distinction between Christianity being a time-based religion—where there's creation and Adam and Even and the coming of Christ and there will be a second coming, so there's a timeline, in contrast to traditional American Indian religions that are based on particular geographic spots. So they are spatial.

LJM: The Sacred Hills, for example, in Don Coldsmith's books.

TEACHING, WRITING, AND BALANCE

LJM: If you could decide exactly how your work life would be, how much time would you spend teaching and how much writing and how much on committees and how much in meetings?

DL: I like teaching. It fuels me. It keeps me in touch with a younger generation, which I'm beginning to appreciate as I'm getting older. I have enough extrovert in my make-up that I really do like getting out, so probably one-third teaching, two-thirds writing would be good.

LJM: That sounds good. What is your next writing project, and then what is your dream project?

DL: My next writing project, I'm a hundred pages into it, and I hope to finish it up by August of '96, is a calendar round. I thought, let's take this European heritage thing and do a day book, and it's called *A Day Book of Interiors*. I'm trying to do an entry for almost every day of the year. I'm into my second year now, so I'm having to fudge on what year it is. I'm maybe going to drop the year so it is an eternal time. I really have enjoyed this day book idea, and then I'm trying to connect that with a place each day.

LJM: Is this prose?

DL: Yes. Though I am trying to kind of spice up the prose and make it poetic.

LJM: I think you don't have to do that. I think Touching the Sky *is a poet writing a prose book. I think there's poetry in that prose. I saw that in the very first section I read.*

DL: I hope so. I would like to write poetry, but it takes a certain kind of concentration that I don't have at this time of my life. I look forward to my fifties.

IV—WORD ALCHEMY

EARTH-CENTERED WRITING:
A Prairielands Alchemy

AN ALCHEMY OF WRITING

INTRODUCTION TO TULIP ELEGIES

Earth-Centered Writing:
A Prairielands Alchemy

When I first planted tulips, I did not expect to learn about alchemy, an old Earth teaching. Yet as I studied connections between medieval European tulips and the occult science, I understood how Old World philosophy relates to my own writing. At the same time, as an inhabitant of North America, I also experience Indigenous American influences. Breathing winds from the Rocky Mountains, drinking water from the Kaw River, warming under the direct prairie sun, and walking on limestone bedrock infuse me with the continent's elements. Native peoples sang, spoke, drew, and envisioned this "new" world for thousands of years. The study of earth's elements is alchemy, whether the ground is Egyptian or Kansan.

As a child, I watched my mother plant tulips in the fall season, in her Great Plains garden, and in my own first garden, almost unconsciously, I imitated her example. I never questioned that I would tend a garden. I later found iris plants at the tombstone of my great-grandmother, dug up a piece, and reset the rhizome beside a pine in my garden, where it blooms every spring. The family gardening heritage, and also perhaps some faint trace of my ancestor's essence from the soil, joins with my daily experience. The matrix of the past creates present life.

That November, when I carved a burrow in the ground for tissue-wrapped bulbs, I could not help but feel, amidst life, I was digging a grave. The husk in my hand seemed to be corpse-like, as lifeless as dry foliage of the fall garden. As I sheered sod, I felt like I was trespassing into the forbidden country of the dead, where centipedes and maggoty, intestine-shaped pieces of life squirmed. The prospect of blood-red springtime blossoms seemed remote. Clay soil was a barren compost, yet I saw how digestion of all surface matter occurs in this middling zone of fungus and worms.

Earth's covering is soil. The Old English word *"eorðe"* means "ground, soil, dry land," and it can be generalized to be a synonym for "material world"—the base below the heavens but above the underworld. This suggests a theological site of thought more than a physical location. Our host planet consists of fire, rock, and then this layer of crumbing bodies. Just an inch below the earth's surface, inexplicable transformations occur. Metaphor and reality merge in this realm, and in the winter, after months of reading, I found the code of thought known as alchemy—a knowledge that persisted alongside Judaism, Christianity, and Islam.

I began writing a set of poems about alchemy, and also about the tulip species, in the sequence *Tulip Elegies*. The tenth section explicitly reflects the connection between the two:

Alchemy means darkness: Khem—
old word for Egypt—means
black earth. Flooded fields
and graves where losses conclude
become the alchemist's furnace,
like Nile floodplain, sun-stewed,
limned with loam and salamanders.
Putreficatio begins

and the King sinks underground.
He joins serpents and worms
and His purple robe blackens.
He roams onyx mansions
and does not see His tears
steamed by sulfur and fire
or a leafy wreath around His head
rise into heaven uncorrupted....

At a literal level, the poem is simply about a tulip bulb coming to life in the spring, and indeed the leaves, or here the "leafy wreath," emerge first, before the bloom. I found "*khem*" comes from the lost Egyptian language, reincarnated into English as the root of "chemistry." The poem acknowledges Egyptian origins of European culture, then continues to the Latin word, *putreficatio,* the dissolution phase of alchemy. The term also implies resurrection, a term that resonates with biblical and other traditions of rebirth. The true mystery in this poem, and in my garden's actual under-surface, is both decay and subsequent reassembly of elements.

My attempt to articulate this simple garden event in "Tulip Elegies X" engages many continents and languages. I did not expect to find the connection to the Nile Valley civilizations when I started this poem, but words, like plants, have deep roots.

Another tradition besides alchemy informs my writing—American In-digenous thought. An example comes from a place name of my home area, the Flint Hills. An early map of Kansas, when the U.S. considered the land "Indian Territory," includes Potawatomi towns. One translates as "Place Scraping the Sky," an image suggesting the immensity of sky. The term describes how landscape, and beings, "scrape" the sky. We walk through the lower stratum of heaven, and our dwellings rise into the atmosphere, yet our feet must always rest on ground. The Potawatomi name further implies the interaction between sky energy and earth energy. Algonquin languages have verb forms embedded within nouns, so a name is an active, ongoing motion, a language alchemy. On the plains, where land stretches to full-circle horizons, both halves of the world find con-stant repositionings.

All physical laws, and perhaps most religious accounts, derive from el-emental marriage of sky and earth. The Potawatomi people knew this, and in ancient Egypt, the sages encoded the same laws into astrology, which is study of the sky, and alchemy, study of the earth.

The unencumbered vista was the best part of growing up in semi-ru-ral Kansas—from glowing Milky Way rivers of stars to turning circles of grassy hills. Bluestem grass on the prairies reach six feet high, and the wind moves the fronds in constant ripples. From sky and earth come the myriad details of this world, or the ten hundred million beings, as the Buddhists say.

My aesthetic derives from Egyptian culture and awareness of Indig-enous American presence, equally as ancient. Both cultures place Sky and Earth at the center.

A nature-based poetics risks pastoralism, a simplistic belief in the good-ness of nature, but no one who survives the grasslands is a fool. To live on the prairie lands and run a ranch and practice agriculture, a person cannot be naïve. To write well about the Flint Hills of Kansas, my home, requires an understanding of the complexities of geography, history, geology, ecology, religion, rhetoric, and poetics. Gary Snyder once described to me the role of the poet as a person who reflects upon cultural and natural experiences and digests them into word compositions. This is the task, to create writings that distill chaos into lyric. Snyder advocated this community-based literature, rather than art for art's sake or art for individual glory and commerce.

As understanding of community grows more sophisticated, through technological archiving of histories, writers have more stored knowledge than ever imagined and greater challenges as writers. When I was growing up in the 1950s and 1960s, much information was already available. I read about Egyptian antiquities in the Emporia public library, where I also found Marie Sandoz's books about Lakota history. I read Mark Twain and Conan books and Freud's books on dreams. At school we read Dickens and George Eliot. On my father's shelves, I found books on Borneo head-hunting and the *Tibetan Book of the Dead*. My grandmother shared poetry of the Chinese and Japanese Zen traditions.

At the same time, I attended the First Congregational Church and sang British hymns. The radio brought African and American-influenced rock and roll to this small town between the Neosho and Cottonwood Rivers. The local music store imported West Coast jazz records along with Stevie Wonder, show tunes, and other pop music. I went to music recitals of Bach and Mozart. Now, fifty years later, even more realities reproduce infinitely in print and electronic media.

Simplistic fundamentalism does not suffice to order this complexity, nor does two-dimensional writing. The times call for an alchemy of writing that reaches deeply into earth and as high into the heavens as electronically assisted sight permits. At first I struggled to corral complexity into site-specific language, as in "Big Springs Cemetery," I once wrote, which did not penetrate enough strata:

This burial hill rises
between Stull and Clinton,
on past the new reservoir
where we hiked all afternoon.
The November wind over
the graves chills the boys.
They hop over the sunken

100

pits of weeds
and race each other to the car
while we step slowly
reading stories from the marble markers.

We look for the oldest dates,
the youngest babies,
the largest family groups,
those names approaching our own.

This poem floats on the surface. It is a silhouette instead of a portrait, like flat metal sculptures, of cowboys roping steers. Without the line breaks, it could be a journal entry. The ending does turn inward, the first shift outside a literal narration. The opportunity missed is the chance to explore layered experiences, in the language itself and in all the histories within the coordinates of month and cemetery.

The writer's challenge is to compress infinite human and natural spheres into the medium of language. The literary tradition itself is elaborate. English texts pay homage to the Egyptians and their alchemy; to the Graeco-Roman philosopher-poets; and to the Judaeo-Christian histories. To this aggregate snowball, add a Viking and French and Latinate language, English, and its texts: Geoffrey Chaucer, who first wrote literature in the rough English vernacular rather than Latin; and Shakespeare; and numerous other British poets and essayists and novelists, who developed English-language genres. Writers inherit the accident of American English, and its earlier practitioners, like Walt Whitman, who developed long poetic lines, and Edgar Allen Poe, who created horror stories, science fiction, detective stories, fantasy, and symbolist poetry. Diverse immigrants to America streamlined grammar and syntax. Algonquin and Iroquoian nations first impacted English speakers and began the process of Native cultural infiltration. Welsh, African-American, German, Mexican, Cherokee, Muskogee, Siouan, English and other settlers founded Emporia and created the first dialect I heard. Other influences I recall are the Osages and Kaw and Chippewa Indian people who lived near Emporia during territorial times; drovers of the Flint Hills and farmers of the Osage Cuestas; and recent Laotian, Vietnamese, and Salvadorian immigrants. Literary figures William Allen White and William Lindsay White, father and son editors of the *Emporia Gazette*, still influence ideas about writing in Emporia. To write well about my hometown, I cannot be simplistic.

As a writer, I must embrace complications: shift among details of place, and then engage in mind-geology. I go prospecting by doing research, and that is another way of loving the myriad details of this world. Reading other poets is a way. One example of a place-conscious, elaborate poet is Kansas-born William Stafford, whose writings journey among geographies and embellish sites with human meaning. I discover, when working with his poems, his ability to find words that act as levers, words that appear ordinary on the surface, but then catapult the mind into unrecognized territory, as in the phrase "fence wire hums" in the poem "Happy in Sunlight":

Maybe it's out by Glass Butte some
time in late fall, and sage owns the whole
world. Even the obsidian chips
left by the Indians glitter, out of
their years. Last night's eager stars
are somewhere, back of the sky.

Nothing where you are says, "It's me
only." No matter how still the day,
a fence wire hums for whatever there is,
even if no one is there. And sometimes
for luck, by neglecting to succeed that day,
you're there, no one else, and the fence wire sings.

The personification of "sage owns" is a reversal, forcing the reader to see from the sage plant's viewpoint, an earth-centered perspective. Stafford collapses time by referencing the "obsidian chips" from stone-working inhabitants of another history, and at the end, time disappears completely, and "you're there." The word "hums" is the pivot of the poem's movement. Every part of the poem's preliminary description leads to that climactic moment.

Stafford is an alchemist. Earth and sky conjoin in the reference to Glass Butte, a landmark, and the sky, "last night's eager stars," which are present if not visible. The poet argues against an egocentric view within this landscape, with the minimal traces of human habitation, but then with "fence wire hums," he centers a manmade object in the equation, so the narrator and the poem's audience ("you") hear not just the "hum" but how "the fence wire *sings*" (my emphasis). This poem brings together the landscape, history, flora, astronomy, barbed wire, and finally a metaphysical leap into another dimension of experience. Wind blowing wire fencing literally does make a singing sound, so the poem has exact literalness, as well.

I learned to listen to Stafford in Emporia, and at the same time I learned to listen to jazz. The town shares a rich Midwestern jazz tradition, as trains and highways carried musicians from Kansas City through Emporia to Wichita on a regular tour. My father played in a Wichita jazz band, and at the College of Emporia, in turn, I learned jazz. At the high school I learned marching music and classical European music. I learned that music is an art that finds form beneath the sky, and then disappears into its reaches. Jazz molds itself to the dimension of time most fluently, I came to believe.

From improvisatory jazz I learned an essential about poetry: timing is everything. Details of poem are a rhythm line, keeping the song in motion. Every so often a soloist can cut loose, with a trumpet melody jumping into high altitudes. That flight can be the moment in Stafford's poem when the time folds inside out. It can be one of John Donne's metaphors, or a glimpse of the Pyramids. It can be the arrow thrust of a tulip's green stem piercing snow. Sky and earth suspend in balance. Then the soloist returns and lands solidly onto rich black soil, and a steady heartbeat resumes. Dimensions of earth and sky, and their infinite interplay, create a dynamic language of alchemy. The writer hopes for such earth music.

Low, Denise. *Tulip Elegies*. Lawrence: Penthe, 1993.

Stafford, William. *Kansas Poems of William Stafford*. Ed. Denise Low. Topeka: Woodley, 1990. P. 11.

An Alchemy of Writing

I. May 26, 1992, Lawrence

November, a difficult time, begins the season of death. Drizzle turns to frost and on the plains, underlaid by flat terraces of limestone cuestas, winds become gales. Plants and animals take cover or die in November, season to pause, to hang in balance between cold and heat, earth and sky, life and death.

In this tidal zone between seasons, certain plants flourish, plants with adaptations to the underground, beyond the reach of frost. Some even birth themselves in the midst of solstice freezes, including bulb plants. Originally bulbs were buds, broken from an extinct ancestral branch. They carry within tiny flowers that will emerge in spring. These buds are armored like mollusks, shaped to burrow in dirt through winter nights.

November of 1989 was particularly difficult for me, with no trace of harvest or spring. My father had had a stroke a few months before that left him paralyzed and mute. When his birthday came on November 6, we understood his damaged mind would not recover. It was excruciating to watch the metamorphosis of a robust man into an invalid. Months later I still felt helpless to correct this catastrophe to my father.

Only in dreams was he whole:

"September 20, 1989. Dream. My father thanks me in a dream for listening to him, for letting him talk."

"October 9, 1989. Dream. My father speaks."

November of 1989 was also the first anniversary of the death of Cecil Dawes, Junior, a student at Haskell Indian Junior College, who died by unknown means. He disappeared for ten awful days. His father's office was next to mine and his mother's across campus, and I participated in their anguish. Soon after his disappearance a Cree medicine man from Canada conducted a ceremony and foresaw the death. Town psychics saw murder and water, but no clear evidence remained when the body finally surfaced in the Kaw River.

Riverwater corrodes tree limbs and shale and flesh equally. The life-giving river became an agent of death for a young man who laughed and ran races and studied hard. He was a descendant of Black Kettle, a member of the Cheyenne and Creek nations, and sorely needed in this world.

He is still missed.

"October 18. Dream. I worry about Cecil, Junior. Where has he gone?"

***

The tulip poems originated in a difficult time, in the difficult mode of language. For me, speech is an awkward medium. The youngest of four children, I could not keep up with the verbal prowess of giants around me. Only when I learned to read did I acquire most words in my vocabulary, by sight, alone. For years I had no idea how to pronounce them. Still, I desperately wanted to be heard. I turned to writing.

Journals are salve for those years. White pages always listen.

In 1989 I had little time to write, so there are many gaps in the journal, and poems do not appear until November. They intermix with reports of my father's small progress, with expressions of guilt and grief, with dreams, with daily affairs. During this time I was commuting three or four days a week to the rehabilitation center in Topeka, after a working day. I was exhausted, with little time for writing down the experiences.

Dreams became important, and many were comforting dreams sent from friends:

"August 30. Dream. We stay with Lois in a house of blue tiles and mists. Her peacefulness spreads to me."

"September 11. Dream. Driving on a New Mexico road to see Luci and Bob. I see water standing on the sides of the road, and tadpoles swimming in a flurry, and an aquatic Gila monster."

"October 3. Dream. We buy Sally and Scott's cabin in Oregon. It is surrounded by exotic forests. We find a mushroom, colored sky-blue and lavender."

Some nights were continuation of grief:
"Dream. Inside a house I burst into tears because of my father."

Grappling with this mythical father-loss engaged me at many levels, and my journal writing became a way of telling my pain: of shaping it and measuring it from different vantage points.

The tulip poems begin in November, my father's seventy-fifth birthday, and continue alongside dreams and reportage for a year. They all share a similar intensity—of colors, of feelings, of images.

The other poems I wrote explicitly about my father's stroke are flat in comparison to them. They felt forced, except for one, "The Language of Aphasia," which centers on the tarot card "The Hanged Man." Imagery of tarot was a pivot in writing about archetypal experience of loss. It provided an aesthetic distance—a language of alchemy and tulips—and a means of symbolic conversation within myself:

Since his stroke it is as though he hangs
upside down, gagged, his four limbs crucified

on the dimensions of time and space. He speaks
only simple syllables, beginning with m-m-m-m

and finishing with open vowels. He has
this survival-level language, a child's

first alphabet to reach for milk or mother—
and with these simple sounds he gropes

to describe the terrain he floats in.
When I promise he will speak again

he shakes his head no. He breathes sounds
through his lips, squeezes them flat

and open, and then stops. I tell him
he will heal and learn speech and one day

rise from the weight of unmovable flesh
where he flounders, struggles for air,

and invents a new vocabulary
as though his life depends on it.

***

I do not want to center my writing on clichés of loss. Everyone loses parents and grandparents. This is always painful.

I turned to writing about early winter because it was the season I surfaced from a nightmare of hospital rooms and tried to respond to exact objects around me. I returned to poet William Carlos Williams: "No ideas but in things." Of course, the previous season had changed what I brought to my writing. It had changed all winters.

***

In rereading the journals, a healing direction emerges, word-maps of dreams and events that become more and more complete. The process of rendering experience into language was navigation through incomprehensible feelings. The named pain in entries, measured and scaled, became more fully delineated. Shadows became lines of definition around objects. A culminating dream was about my grandmother, mother, and sister:

"November, 1989. Dream. In my childhood home, which now has wooden floors, like my present house. My mother and sister are asleep in the back bedroom. The pear tree is visible through the corner window. My grandmother's afghans are in the closet for me to use.

"When I turn from the closet, the room has enlarged. It is airy and sun-filled, and the trunk of the pear tree now grows from the wooden floor. It is covered with nearly ripe fruit."

II. June 6, 1992, Lawrence

Tulips are composed of such universal shapes that literal description blends into metaphor. They are close to organic poetry already.

The blossom is a sphere or circle or cup; the leaves, sometimes ruffled, are elongated triangles, suggesting Trinity. Six petals are the Seal of Solomon or Star of David. Black snake-eyes stamens contrast with saturated crimson or pastel hues. The long stem arrows upward, like the swords of the tarot card deck, complemented by the feminine suit of cups.

Like snakes, tulips begin life in the underworld, and indeed flourish in the land of the dead. Underground mother bulbs are wombs among decay of other beings. Like all plants and everything living, they transform the past into future.

After writing the second tulip poem, I recognized the imagery alluded to something beyond gardens and nature. I had read alchemy briefly in my twenties and still owned Titus Burkhardt's *Alchemy: Science of the Cosmos, Science of the Soul*. Also, I found a picture of a 16ᵗʰ century scene from Turkey: a group of a dozen men around a huge tulip replica, and a smaller caduceus next to it. The caduceus was three entwined snakes, symbol of healing and of Egyptian Hermetic mysteries. In front of the crowd of turbaned onlookers was a man wearing an Egyptian headdress with a curved cobra at the forehead. He carried a staff, like Moses, and he bent at the waist in a ritualized gesture. The circle of men around the tulip and caduceus emphasized their interrelationship. I examined this picture many times over the months of writing the poems, and its imagery is an important source for the writing.

The direction of the tulip elegies became more consciously aligned with iconography of alchemy.

***

Alchemy is about spiritual process, not primitive chemistry or metallurgy. The alchemical tradition is from a time of no distinction between sacred and secular, when the four elements—earth, air, water, and fire—behaved in meaningful patterns. The cosmic egg was still intact. Richard Grossinger writes about a "simultaneity" not unlike Carl Jung's idea of synchronicity; alchemy is: "A method of symbolism working on the simultaneity of a series of complementary pairs:

Sun/Moon,
Gold/Silver,
Sulfur/Mercury,
King/Queen,
Male/Female,
Husband/Bride,
and Christ/Man."

The members of a pair work together in a balance, not in opposition. Nothing is born or killed, only expressed in new ways: "Dissolution of any formal entity is but the preparation for a new conjunction between a forma and its material" (Burkhardt).

A tulip growing, blooming, and wilting fulfills alchemical law.

My father and mother, my king and queen of childhood years, have changed dozens of times. My father was transformed again after his stroke, and the change may have a spiritual aspect not apparent at first. The end of one phase of life signals the beginning of another, and the ultimate outcome is a mystery.

Dreams take form from unknown *materia*.

Journal entries take unexpected turns.

A potent force field interpenetrates the visible world, an invisible Twin/ Gemini, Messenger/Hermes force. It enables dream stories to arise from the unconscious; it connects sounds to words; it allows premonitions, intuitions, and prophecies to move along a net of silent interconnections.

III. June 6, 1992, Lawrence, June 17, 1992, Berkeley,
June 24-5, 1992, Lawrence
Today, June 6, the sun aligns with the constellation Gemini, and I write all morning, pen tracing circles and lines of letters. The words are symbols of spirit (circles) and matter (lines), *materia* and *forma*.

Letters of the alphabet are very old, and I use these relics of Phoenician traders and Egyptian priests to form a new day, a new incarnation of Mercury/Hermes.

Roland Barthes writes "words have a second-order memory, which mysteriously persists in the midst of new meanings"; this is also true of written words, derived from Egyptian hieroglyphic, hieratic, and demotic scripts, as well as Semitic variations. The correspondence in these languages between sounds and letters is more direct: *aleph* is "ox" in Egyptian and Semitic languages; the letter A is an inverted head of an ox.

Greeks took the letter A to represent only the sound A, which is unrelated to the Greek words for ox, *tauros* and *bous*. But vestiges of the mother script remain: M derives from "mu," for "water"; T comes from "taw," for "mark."

An Egyptian bull god incarnates into English script every time capital A is printed and read.

The font of this very text is called "Roman," dating to two thousand years ago when Roman sculptors adapted Egyptian-Semitic-Greek letters to stone monument engraving. They straightened curves to fit their chisels. The Roman alphabet contains arrows (Z), the Nile (M), eyes of Horus (O), snakes (N), boomerangs (C), temple doors (D), and persons in prayer (E). These letters evoke an old magic.

Ultimately, letters have sacred origins in Egypt, in the teachings of Egyptian priests who worshipped Thoth and his female counterpart Seshat. Texts of Thoth and Seshat were honored in ceremonial processions, beginning the Western tradition of religious text.

Symbolic scripts for alchemy, astrology, and the alphabet all derive from Egyptian religion. Astrology and alchemy together represent the whole cosmos—heaven and earth—and the alphabet is the imprint of human thought moving between the two.

Alchemical symbols overlap with astrological ones, most notably Mercury and Quicksilver, the only symbol to include all three components of circle, crescent, and cross. The circle is heaven and the cross earth, and the manifest world is shadings of the two.

Letters and alchemical symbols are made of the same writing system, the same lineage from *Khem,* land of dark soil, Egypt. The mysterious force that binds meaning and symbol is the Azoth, "universal life force" (Hall).

***

Tulip plants correspond to alchemical imagery:

Buds	Cosmic egg—"inner space of the soul."
	Spheres of planets, moon and earth.
	Globes.
	Jeweled Orb, held in the king's hand.
	Eyes—windows to look outward or inward.
Blossoms	Circles of the Ptolemaic heavens, paths of the planets.
	Ouroboros, snake of time consuming itself.
	Ouroboros, dragon-serpent, tail in mouth - turning within.
	Spiral paths around a mountain.
	Sun—pure light, spirit.
	Crown.
	Chalice or cup or flask—place of alchemical fusion.
Plant	Tree of life.
	Alchemical marriage of male and female—completion.
Springtime	Bloom time.
	Aries—beginning of the zodiac year.

Easter, resurrection.
Conjunction.
Fulfillment of time: inception, coagulation, and dissolution.
Once upon a time.
A story begins within a segment of time.

IV. *May 29, 1992, Lawrence*

The process of writing the tulip poems was deeply satisfying, as I can express myself in writing beyond my ability to speak. Writing extends the capabilities of my mind: ideas can be invented, destroyed, shaped, and preserved in a particular plane of time.

Walter Ong writes about the necessary characteristics of orally preserved literatures: the need for mnemonic devices of parallelism, repetition, and rhyme.

Certainly oral traditions that have developed for centuries do have complex literatures and histories. Navajo ceremonies like the Blessing Way take days to complete, with memorized songs that must be sung correctly. African historians recount days-long histories. In this tradition the literature is a compendium of communal experience and wisdom.

Other kinds of oral literatures are individually creative, like storytelling, where sometimes a plot line is already known, but descriptive details, pacing and digressions are part of an artful performance. The experience of sound, though, is transient, and no performance is ever exactly repeated. Dennis Tedlock invented a typographic alphabet of Zuni storytelling to represent sound, like a musical score, but it is limited by its inability to reflect improvisation.

For me, writing with pen and paper is a silent performance. The tools of language enact the mental state: physical text-making delineates thought into physical being, with allowance for elaboration, discovery and revision. Like beadwork, patterns can be seen and then amended: more subordination, more digression, elaboration, qualifications, shadings. With ongoing revision, writing is improvisational, until a final version results. Only the end product of writing is static.

William Stafford explains writing as a process of spontaneous discovery:

A writer is not so much someone who has something to say as he is someone who has found a process that will bring about new things he would not have thought of if he had not started to say them.

111

V. May 31, 1992, Lawrence

Transcendent sensations can be activated by great art. Dante, William Shakespeare, and Rainer Maria Rilke all produced multiphonic works, which speak to all ears of the body. Body, mind and soul are all engaged, so a person is fully alive.

Valery writes about the potential of poetry, as it "co-ordinates the greatest number of independent parts or factors: sound, sense, the real and the imaginary, logic, syntax, and the double invention of content and form. . . ." Spectators become actors, with imagination, senses, intellect, and intuition all brought to life.

The best artists hew patterns of sensations across dimensions, at once emotional, intellectual, and spiritual.

***

Kurt Vonnegut proposes that reading books is the Western form of meditation. Unlike orthodox traditions of meditation, which require withdrawal from society, reading joins two minds, and in fact readers have access to the greatest minds in history, through their remaining texts. Their ideas and language patterns, even in imperfect translations, still induce mirrored states of thought.

***

Sappho greets anyone alive who has eyes to read. She entrances us one by one.

Her words last imperfectly, with lacunae, but still preserved, copied in exact ink. Her body long since has returned to the elements. Only her lettered thoughts endure.

***

The moments I was immersed in writing the *Tulip Elegies* was the first peace I experienced after my father's crippling stroke. The writings and rewritings engaged me for weeks at a time in a healing trance.

VI. May 31, 1992, Lawrence

Visual patterns can have powerful impact on the ordering of mind. A flame or blossom has a calming effect because its natural symmetry is replicated by the act of visualization.

Colors have similar effect at the most organic, pre-verbal level, absorbed through the simple reptile brain.

Think of sky-blue. Green. Lavender.

A regular count of syllables in a line of poetry sets up an order. Drum and flute echo in curved ears and hit the thin membrane of eardrum.

Then magic.

***

Another aspect of language script: words as amulets:

Orthodox Jews strap small bundles of scripture, t'filin, on their heads: Thou Shalt Love The Lord Thy God With All Thy Heart With All Thy Soul And With All Thy Might.

Egyptians covered coffins with spells from the Book of the Dead, to help souls pass through the stages of the Underworld. Decans of the Egyptian zodiac etched on stone coffins showed the path through heaven. Later, Ptolemaic Egyptians still inscribed spells on tablets and stones and paper, in demotic Greek.

Mayans covered public buildings, monuments, steles, caves, vases, jewelry and books. Their script was composed of both sacred iconography and phonetic abstractions. At seasonal ceremonies priests declared prayers written on bark paper, the sounds rising with copal incense smoke to heavens filled with gods.

Sanskrit syllables are sacred in both written and sounded forms, with associations with the chakras. They are enacted as both mantras and mandalas, the best known being OM, or AUM, or AMEN.

Tibetan prayer wheels, spun only clockwise, imprint the air with raised letters of prayers. Sutras printed on thin paper are folded into hollow, gilt Buddhas, along with seeds.

***

Despite the commercialization of language by the advertising industry, all language—written, spoken, or mediated—has a sacred potential, the ordering of chaos.

A first line of poetry codifies the physics of a discrete new dimension. The proposed world of a poem is not only a mental construct, but also stirs inner sensations of spirit. Language patterns unify breath, heartbeat, and reflection.

Words are individual stones in a bridge between two people, writer and reader.

Two lovers.

The sequence of generations.

VII. May 31, 1992, Lawrence
  Surviving fragments of Heraclitus.
  Sappho's verse.
  The silence of lacunae in broken texts
  Hamlet. King Lear. The Tempest.
  "Ode to a Nightingale." "Ode on a Grecian Urn."
  The poetry of Rainer Maria Rilke.
  My grandmother's love of Li Po and Tu Fu.
  Prayers in Kiowa. Prayers in Cherokee.
  Ponca songs. The Night Hawks singers and drummers.
  Schiller's "Ode to Joy." Beethoven.
  A phoebe singing its call notes at twilight.
  Light rain falling, palms of leaves collecting the drops.

VIII. June 1, 1992, Lawrence

My love of plants comes from two accidents of birth. I was born in a small town surrounded by tall grass prairie, and I was born to a mother who loved plants.

Two-hundred species grow in Lyon County, at the edge of the Flint Hills. In unplowed prairie the species are evenly dispersed, so each season brings to life a new wave of wildflower colors. A variety of tuberous plants, grasses, shrubby plants, shallow-rooted and deep-rooted plants, mushrooms, and bulbs grow in equilibrium. These plants embody their own form of intelligence: compass plant leaves always align with North; sunflowers follow the daily route of the sun.

Every vacant lot in town reverted to dense foliage if left unmowed. The pattern of houses and streets was interrupted by resurgences of prairie in yards, drainage ditches, even cracks in the red brick streets. Animal beings of the prairie were ever present at the back door: garter snakes, mice, birds, rabbits, squirrels, opossum, spiders, fireflies, toads, geckos.

More plants were brought with European immigrants—my assorted great-great-grandparents—who also had notions of English and continental gardening. The climate allowed certain adaptations of roses, daisies, daffodils, iris, lilies, and tulips. Each spacious yard was cultivated according to heritage and whim: a side yard of bachelor button pastels; a collection of hybridized iris; hedges of voluptuous peonies; ferns along a house foundation. I loved the sense of exotica created by each garden.

My mother happened to garden; she mothered her plants with single-minded fervor. She planted and then uprooted a willow. She planted hens-and-chickens outside my window, along with grape hyacinths and iris. She dug out a level surface and laid shale flagstones. Asparagus grew wild in the back garden, behind the grapevines and strawberries.

My mother told me women who garden know how to accept their aging. They know the life cycles, birth to death.

She taught me unusual names for plants: coreopsis, hyacinth, ajuga, coleus, phlox, flax, vinca, iris, pansy, narcissus, caladium, trillium, and tulip. I also learned ordinary names: honeysuckle, spearmint, lemon balm, jack-in-the-pulpit, forget-me-not.

Tulips were as common in spring as neighborhood cats.

I started writing about tulips in 1989, after I planted a set of Queen Elizabeth tulips, with trowel and bone meal in hand.

At planting I thought of Susan Fromberg Schaeffer's poems "T" and "Tulips Again." Memories of those poems converged with the moment, along with hopes for the year to come.

If God did die

And left something behind,
Surely he left these tulips
These crazy women of womb shapes....
                    ("Tulips Again")
                ***

All winter,
They lie in the black earth.
They are blind in the eyes.

Their sleep more deep
Than the dead.
They sleep without dreams

For they save themselves up.
Then,
Something touches them.

Their dark wombs open....("T")

IX. June 7, 1992, Lawrence

I write this recollection of November, 1989, during the spring season, as the sun rises earlier every day, and daylight expands into long dawns and twilights. Birds begin a clamor at 5:00 in the morning. Tulips in my yard are dormant, with just a few scraps of papery debris left. But as solstice comes closer, most plants flourish in the warmth and humidity. Green frames every view outdoors: trees at the skyline, bushes, vines, more trees, grass underfoot, flowers in boxes and pots.

My father, a Scorpio, born in November, endures, different from the man he was before. He listens and laughs occasionally, but still cannot talk. I watch his eyes more, facial expressions, and gestures of his left hand. He seems unaware of the right side of his body, and blind to it, but the left side is strong. Without words, his presence has become more intense, like his new persona in my dreams. When we part, he presses my hand hard, and we connect in a more peaceful way.

My mother cares for him, with help, and she is exhausted. They have been married fifty-six years, living in tandem, their birthdays only ten days apart. Her life has been completely altered by his disability.

Nonetheless, she continues to tend iris and a collection of two-hundred varieties of day lilies. She writes:

"June 5, 1992. The iris bloomed tall and beautiful. Day lilies are starting —lots of stems and buds, almost solid in back—will probably have to think about dividing before long."

***

I do not compose these sentences quickly; time is needed for processing images and emotions. Words are letter-bundles made of imperfectly balanced elements and fragmentary glyphs. I rework them with imperfect memories to approximate experiences of 1989 and of now. Many voices join with mine.

Fall and spring fit together with past and present.

I keep writing other entries in the journal, too, including a new sequence of dreams:

"June 5, 1992. Dream. A certain medicine man comes by my porch. My husband and I spread red blankets for him. He continues South of the house to perform a ceremony with many garter snakes. I am glad to be included."

116

"June 1, 1992. Dream. I birth a baby boy. I look for baby clothes and find a closet in my childhood house. My mother has kept my old clothes, including a pink-and-blue tweed sweater, the colors of both boys and girls knitted together."

I do not understand the dreams, but they haunt me all day. They speak in their own alphabet, and they spell out the alchemy of my psychology. According to Grossinger, "they are the active means whereby the self creates the grounds of its own existence, the precise psychochemistry of that occurrence."

This writing is another cycle, another attempt to understand why tulips grow in round shapes, how my father's life has changed, and why, one day, after many changes, I too will pass into an unknown season.

***

From Janus Lacinius Therapus, the Calabrian, alchemist:

Three measures must be served in our art:

the first is to know thoroughly the elements, their many names and traditions...

the second is to work continuously, allowing each process to flow over into the next...

the third is to cultivate a patience, a faith based on knowledge of the stars and sun and the works of time: the rhythms and cycles of Nature contain the code and root of our handiwork.

***

Wylma and Cecil Dawes adopted a baby last spring, Chabon Stephen Dawes. His parents and sister tend him carefully. He has a strong spiritual presence centered within activity of a child's body.

Bacher, Elman. *Studies in Astrology, Vol. 6.* Oceanside: Rosicrucian Fellowship, 1965.

Barthes, Roland. "From Writing Degree Zero." *A Barthes Reader.* Ed. Susan Sontag. New York: Hill and Wang, 1983. 37.

Beck, Peggy and Anna L. Walters. *The Sacred: Ways of Knowledge, Sources of Life.* Tsaile, Az.: Navajo Community College P, 1977.

Burkhardt, Titus. *Alchemy: Science of the Cosmos, Science of the Soul.* Baltimore: Penguin Books, 1967. 155, 78.

Crockett, James Underwood. *Bulbs.* Alexandria, VA: Time-Life, 1971.

Cumont, Franz. *Astrology and Religion among the Greeks and Romans.* New York: Dover, 1960.

Dotson, Dorothy. Letter. June 5, 1992.

Egyptian Mythology. New York: Tudor Publishing Co., 1965.

Fagan, Cyril. *Zodiacs Old and New: A Probe into Antiquity.* Los Angeles: Llewellyn Foundation for Astrological Research, 1950.

Grossinger, Richard. "Alchemy: Pre-Egyptian Legacy, Millennial Promise." *The Alchemical Tradition in the Late Twentieth Century.* Ed. Richard Grossinger. Berkeley: North Atlantic Books, 1983. 241, 290.

Hall, Manly Palmer. *The Secret Teachings of All Ages.* Los Angeles: Philosophical Research Society, 1971. CLV.

Kristeva, Julia. "The Novel as Polylogue." *Desire in Language: A Semiotic Approach to Literature and Art.* New York: Columbia U P, 1980.

Lacinius, Janus. "A Form and Method of Perfecting Base Metals." *The Alchemical Tradition in the Late Twentieth Century.* Ed. Richard Grossinger. Berkeley: North Atlantic Books, 1983. 69.

Low, Denise. "The Language of Aphasia." *Cottonwood* #45 (Fall 1991) 7.

McClean, Adam. *The Alchemical Mandala.* Grand Rapids, Mich.: Planes Press, 1989.

Naylor, P.L.H. *Astrology: A Fascinating History.* N. Hollywood: Wilshire Book Co., 1967.

Ong, Walter. *Orality and Literacy.* London: Methuen, 1982.

Schaeffer, Susan Fromberg. *Alphabet for the Lost Years.* San Francisco: Gallimaufry, 1976."T," "Tulips Again," n.p.

Stafford, William. *Writing the Australian Crawl.* East Lansing: Michigan St. U Press, 1982.

Tedlock, Dennis. *Finding the Center: Narrative Poetry of the Zuni Indians.* Lincoln and London: U of Nebraska Press, 1972.

Valery, Paul. "Poetry and Abstract Thought." *Paul Valery: An Anthology.* Ed. James R. Lawler. London and Henley: Routledge and Kegan Paul, 1977. 165.

Vonnegut, Kurt. Address. University of Kansas. Lawrence, 1987.

World Book Encyclopedia. Chicago: Field Enterprises.

Tulip Elegies

I.
November, season to aim
the spade and bear down hard.
Grass gives, rips open:
sod and black flesh.
From crumbled stone will rise
the new year. I bury
crisp buds into the breach
and press them further down.
Decay surrounds these children
all winter like memory surrounds
each moment. Next March

shining petals will carry
a core of darkness up from subsoil.
Sun will loosen wrappings of crimson
and tulips will show open hands,
empty, as though nothing spun
in their centers all those months.
Skin and layers of muscles enfold
the same spinning shadow,
the mystery passed from parents
to children, in far places,
in graveyards where life begins.

II.
Geese bleat over the roof, conversing
somehow with stars as we drowse
beneath constellations of beating wings.
Rearranging staggered lines they steer
a sunward pattern, calling out
as they fly, naming the long way.

Below, under shovels of dirt
the dead move imperceptibly,

turning into other shapes of life.
Tulip bulbs shift under dark horizons
of winter and wedge against years
of decayed shale. Shoots form within,
still trapped, and a miniature blossom
waits in each bleached kernel. Last spring
winged leaves fed this future and wilted.
Now, unmoved by geese or moonlight,
bulbs listen through solstice nightfall
for the searing call of one hot star.

III.
Some of the bulbs interred last fall
with handfuls of bone meal will freeze.
I held each bundle—paper wrapped
around pear-white flesh—and set
each into cold soil to grow or die.
Now, in a winter room, under quilts,
I touch my husband's longing. I understand

nothing about this, not the tulips
settling underground and maybe kindling roots
nor the magic pull, like lodestones,
that draws my husband to me each night.
Wound between sheets, skin laid against skin,
we create heat and salt and quiet deaths:
unseen children bleed away. Still

at the center of midnight we come alive
and sense the force that creates us
and geese and next summer's grass and one day
will pull us down into dark histories.
Formless, we become more like a tone
bowed on a cello, *sostenuto*. At solstice
nothing appears to live as wind scours
the hard rim of ground. The new year,
buried below the frostline, is imagined,

is a small hope no larger than my hand.

IV.
Each stalk forms itself
with the symmetry of Bach,
pulls green blood up
into latticework of cells—
augers headfirst
into windy blast
and sun dazzle.
Relieved of the burden
of soil, hard-edged
ruffles relax
and uncover their end—
the single striated bud.

The blossom will balance
over earth, stiff stamens
and smudge of pollen
within a heart-red cup,
the shape composed
to fit between stars

and rock hinterland
where bulbs vibrate
unseen, unheard,
earth-anchored.
The planet's fiery center
pulls, contrapuntal
to the thrust of growth.
It holds fast
each stem aimed
into weightless sky.

V.
This shining in my chest—
familiar, painful, a yearning

to bust loose from skin
wrapped around me long ago
like pearl around a seed
yet the luminance is turned
inward some fire hung
between my throat and belly
to burn and pull me onward
to a lover and to children:
the part of me most unseen
and most potent.

The one-chambered tulip bulb
becomes an ember underground,
a charged lump within pieces of dirt.
From one milky center
covered by tunic and scales
will explode a full-grown plant,
a replica of Dutch ancestors
and Turkish "turban" flowers.

A tracing of its pattern hovers, invisible,
the arabesque of growth held ready
for when the sun turns North again
and sets continents ablaze with petals.
*

Each funeral ends and we remain
alive, with each other, still
in love, still held together
in a veined framework assembled
from old stars. This existence
is not our choice, nor are the sun
and ground we live between.
The burning in each of us—
dormant bulb or human heart—
strains beyond lips and fingers,
beyond evenings spent together
talking into the quiet evening.

The desire to change soil
into petals, that certainty
seared into the oldest bulbs,
is familiar, is a charge
even in my red pulse,
a passion in sap or blood:
I cannot sleep alone.
My shape carries a heat within,
counted out in rhythms when we kiss
and when springtime, I see
a fresh tulip—scarlet, full-fired.

VI.
Vial of saturated color
sculpted from peat,

red red after winter light.
Curio: emperor's tulip.

Living Fabergé egg
rubied by dawn.

Aphrodisiac for the sight
and light touch.

Most perfect lover,
softest lipped, fullest curved.

Centered in the garden
or elevated over bread and meat:

ornament of symmetry
domesticated to fit my hand,

to fill my table with solid
geometry and music.

Fragment of sunset
still radiant at midnight.
Faceted garnet. Tamed dragon.
Catch—of my breath.

VII. *Tulipa hermetica*
The caduceus of lily-flowered tulips
rises from ancient humus—
a bouquet of stems and black eyes—
and renews the memory of gods.
Petals collect particles of gold
by day, dark silver by night,
then shatter back into earth.

Below, where serpents nest,
all the dead intone one word:
everlasting. Without stars,
time erodes like granite.
Roots seine the underworld
and gather strength for
the yearly pilgrimage to light.

Each year's sun moves quickly.
Emerald daggers pierce sediment,
burst into red petals and die
while hidden bulbs swell with buds.
Two-bodied tulip, hermaphrodite,
weds sky and black earth,
mortal blooms and eternity.

VIII.
Resurrection is a falsehood.
The Danish man buried in peat—
stomach filled with spring seeds,
cord around his neck—did not rise
and return to his old mother.
Only barley and rye came to life

as swampwater seeped into his veins.

The *penitente* in New Spain
nailed to a pinewood cross
as cousins guard the highway—
this young man will not revive,
gash himself again with thorns
and offer blood rosaries to Mary.
His last sight will be red dirt,

particles of mountains and roots
stewed together with snowmelt.
Mud is where miracles occur,
where blossoms, kings, and wolves
come apart in final union.
Last Year's tulips disassemble
with stripped bones and clay.

New buds this spring are not
the same flowers resurrected.
They are strangers, never before
seen, born just this once.
Petals are fragile butterflies,
brief spans of tissue to measure
only a half-moon life.

Bulbs live on below, secret,
safe but alone, mothers
who sacrifice all their children
while they become hard knots
and endure. Each year they barter
with the dead around them, swell
with new hope and wait.

IX.
A place camouflaged
by summer grasses,

but underground, hidden:
a fairy ring of spores.
Mussel-shaped buds
folded within tulip bulbs,
embedded in haunted gardens.

*

Snakeholes shaped by stems, abandoned,
running sap dissolved.
Tunnels carved out
like dry creekbeds,
storms ended, twisted
by single-minded current.

*

Not simply a wizened husk
and pulp, but some future
wound into a vegetable
locket, some clock
waiting to be unsprung
by cold hours, water,
a star's close pass.

*

Ghost stems and flowers
left to hover
among chilled roots.
This black season:
muffled sleet above,
hard frozen roof,
and within—held breath.

X.
Alchemy means darkness: *Khem*—
old word for Egypt—means
black earth. Flooded fields
and graves where losses conclude
become the alchemist's furnace,
like Nile Floodplain, sun-stewed,
limned with soil and salamanders.

Putreficatio begins

and the King sinks underground.
He joins serpents and worms
and His purple robe blackens.
He roams onyx mansions
and does not see His tears
steamed by sulfur and fire
or a leafy wreath around His head
rise uncorrupted into heaven.

From hell He calls to the sky
but His lips cannot make sound.
His body has turned invisible
except in shadings of black:
in oakwood smoke, in grooves
of carved stone, in inkwells,
within closed books. Inside
dark blood He pounds and pounds.

Denise Low has taught creative writing at the University of Richmond, Haskell Indian Nations University, and the University of Kansas. Her books include *Touching the Sky: Essays,* (Penthe Press); *A Thailand Journal* (Woodley Press-Washburn University); *New and Selected Poems 1980-1999* (Penthe Press); *Tulip Elegies* (Cottonwood-University of Kansas), *Starwater* (Cottonwood-University of Kansas), and others.

She has won awards and fellowships from the Lannan Foundation, Roberts Foundation National Writing Competition, Academy of American Poet's Pammi-Jurassi Award, Kansas Arts Commission, National Endowment for the Humanities, The Newberry Library, and the Lawrence Arts Commission. She has a PhD from the University of Kansas and an MFA from Wichita State University. Recent publications include reviews in *North Dakota Quarterly, Kansas City Star,* and *Bloomsbury Review;* articles in *Arts & Letters, Studies in American Indian Literature,* and *Midwest Quarterly;* and poems in *Chariton Review, Connecticut Review, I-70, Coal City Review, Mid-America Poetry Review, North American Review,* and *South by Southeast.*

She lives in Lawrence, Kansas with her husband Thomas Pecore Weso and stepdaughter Pemy Wesosa Fleuker. Her children are David Low and Daniel Low.

Also of interest from the Ice Cube Press
the Harvest Book Series—exploring ties between the
spirit of place and our souls.

Prairie Weather (2005), $10.00, 1-888160-17-9
Stories, thoughts and experiences of tornadoes, snow, wind, rain and other
forms of Midwestern weather with Jim Heynen, Mary Swander, Scott
Cawelti, Robert Sayre, Amy Kolen, Debra Marquart, Thomas Dean, Ron
Sandvik, Patrick Irelan and a foreword by Denny Frary.

Living With Topsoil (2004), $9.95 1-888160-99-3
Explorations into our region's world famous topsoil from pears and cabbage
to fossils of the Devonian. Mary Swander, Connie Mutel, Larry Stone,
Timothy Fay, Thomas Dean, Patrick Irelan and Michael Carey.

Finding The Center of the World (2003), $10.95, 1-888160-05-5
Essay on prairie patriotism, place-based poetry and photography by Peter
Bakken as well as poetry by hospital chaplain Nancy Cogan and photos
by Rod Strampe.

The Good Earth: Three Poets of the Prairie (2002)
$9.95, 1-888160-09-8
Explorations of prairie poetry by Paul Engle, William Stafford and James
Hearst with Robert Dana, Denise Low and Scott Cawelti. "These poems are
astonishingly good!"—*Wapsipinicon Almanac*

Prairie Roots: Call of the Wild (2001), $10.95, 1-888160-12-8
Explorations into the muse of the wild: from choosing to be a naturalist,
examining prairie landscape art, following the flight of geese, or trying to
make sense of quirky characters to thinking about the grid system laid across
our land (there's even a small glimpse of giant worms). Paul Gruchow, Robert Sayre, Joni Kinsey, Mary Swander, Thomas Dean, Steve Semken & photos by Howard Vrankin.

Tin Prayer: Words of the Wolverine (2000), $11.95, 1-888160-01-2
A testament to Iowa and the value of natural prayers. Written by Steve
Semken while writer-in-residence at the Island Institute in Sitka, Alaska.

The Ice Cube Press began publishing in 1993 to focus on how to best live with the natural world. Since this time we've been recognized by a number of well known writers including Gary Snyder, Gene Logsdon, Wes Jackson & Barry Lopez. We've published a fair number of well known authors too, including Mary Swander, Jim Heynen, Paul Gruchow. Check out our books at our web site and see why we are dedicated to "hearing the other side."

Ice Cube Press 205 N Front Street
North Liberty, Iowa 52317-9302
p 319/626-2055 f 413/451-0223
steve@icecubepress.com
ॐ
www.icecubepress.com

Printed in the United States
40513LVS00004B/445-486